THE
BIBLE
ENCOUNTERS

THE BIBLE ENCOUNTERS

21 stories of changed lives

THOMAS L. YOUNGBLOOD
SANDRA PICKLESIMER ALDRICH

FOREWORD *by* LEE STROBEL

GRAND RAPIDS, MICHIGAN 49530 USA

ZONDERVAN™

The Bible Encounters
Copyright © 2002 by Sandra P. Aldrich and Tom Youngblood

Requests for information should be addressed to:

Zondervan, *Grand Rapids, Michigan 49530*

Library of Congress Cataloging-in-Publication Data

Youngblood, Thomas L., 1950-
     The Bible encounters : 21 stories of changed lives / Thomas L.
  Youngblood and Sandra Picklesimer Aldrich.
          p. cm.
     ISBN 0-310-24662-8
     1. Bible—Reading. 2. Christian biography. I. Aldrich, Sandra
  Picklesimer. II. Title
  BS617.Y65 2001
  220'.1'32—dc21
  {B}   2002005294

Published in association with the literary agency of Alive Communications, Inc., 7680 Goddard Street, Suite 200, Colorado Springs, CO 80920.

Interior design by Tracey Moran

Printed in the United States of America

---

02 03 04 05 06 07 08 /❖ DC/ 10 9 8 7 6 5 4 3 2 1

Contents

Foreword

Irrelevant. Unreliable. Inaccurate. Confusing. Outdated. Self-contradicting. Fodder for the stupid, the gullible, and the desperate.

That was my opinion of the Bible back when I was an atheist. Had I read and analyzed its contents? No, I was merely reacting to stereotypes about it. Frankly, I wanted as little to do with the Bible as possible.

Then my agnostic wife became a follower of Jesus. As she began praying each day for her hard-hearted, hard-headed husband, the Bible became her refuge. She found hope for me in the words of Ezekiel 36:26: "I will give you a new heart and put a new spirit in you; I will remove from you your heart of stone and give you a heart of flesh."

Intrigued by positive changes in her character and values, I decided to use my journalism and legal training to investigate whether there was any credibility to Christianity. I began to read the Bible, and slowly my conclusions started to change. I became convinced that Christianity is based on a reliable foundation of historical truth and that the Bible possesses a grandeur, a relevance, and a power unlike anything I had ever experienced. I found Hebrews 4:12 to be true: the Bible *is* "living and active" and "it judges the thoughts and attitudes of the heart."

Compelled by the evidence, I finally put my faith in Jesus. Leslie's prayers were answered as he began to transform my heart, my desires, my worldview, my priorities, and my relationships. Over time, I experienced firsthand the power of Scripture to revolutionize a life. Today, the Bible feeds my soul (Psalm 119:103); gives me hope (Romans 15:4); purifies me (Psalm 119:9); teaches me (2 Chronicles 17:9); assures me of eternal life (1 John 5:13); and has become the object of my intense and loving study (Acts 17:11).

Through the years I have continued to be awed as I've watched over and over again how God has used his Word to influence the lives and destinies of human beings. Now my friend Tom Youngblood has partnered with Sandra Aldrich to compile an inspiring series of stories that describe how the power of Scripture has impacted people in a wide variety of ways. As I read their work, I was incredibly encouraged, motivated, inspired, and challenged.

This wonderful book will teach you about God, deepen your confidence in Scripture, and give you practical tools for applying biblical truth to your everyday life. And if you're like me, the first thing you'll do when you put it down will be to thank God for the way he has chosen to use his Word to both mark and mold the lives of his children.

Lee Strobel
Author, *The Case for Christ* and *The Case for Faith*

Letter to the Reader

Dear Reader,

   The power of God's Word. As Christians, we have heard that phrase many times. But what does it really mean? When I think of power, some of the following words come to mind: *horsepower,* as in the Vortec 6 cylinders under the hood of my new car; *wind,* as in the force behind a tropical storm or hurricane like Mitch that recently made landfall; *earthquakes* that destroyed homes and buildings in India and El Salvador; the *evil* power that devastated the World Trade Center in New York City; or the *influence* of an individual to control and make decisions for good or bad.

   Interestingly, all of these forces are measurable. For a six-cylinder engine, 270 horsepower is pretty good since it allows us to climb hills and pass other cars safely. The wind speed behind a hurricane helps us anticipate the potential danger of the storm. The Richter scale helps determine the might of the rolling earth during an earthquake. The total devastation of buildings and loss of life measures the evil of terrorism. The influence of leaders and rulers for good and bad can be measured by the economy, peace, and other indicators of satisfaction in life.

   However, unless power is connected, there seems to be very little we can measure. If my foot never connects to the accelerator in my car, I will never measure the speed of that V6 Vortec engine. If the hurricane never makes landfall, there is little to measure. The earthquakes that happen routinely under the ocean floor are rarely heard of since they have not made connection to where we have property and homes. The influence of evil and terrorism had been somewhat ignored until it connected to landmark buildings in our nation on September 11, 2001. And we will always remember where we were when we heard the news of that connection.

So it is with the power of God's Word. It can be measured when it connects with lives—when people encounter God through his Word. The stories you are about to read reflect the power of God's Word when real people encounter the living God in Scripture. And they all remember where they were in life's journey when they heard in a real and personal way the Good News of that connection to God through Jesus Christ.

I fondly recall growing up in a Christian family in western Pennsylvania and I can't remember not having a Bible—ever. One summer, an older cousin bragged about how many chapters he had read that week in his Bible. I was ready to take on the challenge, but as a thirteen-year-old trying to plow through the version I owned, I found it to be real KGB stuff! Then my Grandma Youngblood gave me a new Billy Graham edition of *Living Letters,* which was a portion of the Scriptures that had been paraphrased by Kenneth Taylor. Suddenly, the Word came alive, and I was excited about what I was reading and how I could apply the principles to my young life.

I still have that old copy of *Living Letters* inscribed with the 1963 date that says, "To Tommy, from Grandma and Granddad." A few years ago, after I had become friends with Kenneth Taylor, I asked him to sign below my grandmother's inscription.

What about the first Bible that made a difference in your life? Where did it come from? Who gave it to you? What caused you to open those pages? Was it because of the person who gave you the gift? Or did the circumstances of your life compel you to begin reading? Ponder that connection for a moment.

In my travels throughout the world, I have seen repeatedly the difference God's Word has made in the lives of individuals who were in desperate situations. I have seen the impact of God's Word in the lives of ministry leaders. In fact, this book is a collection of narrative stories based on people my coauthor, Sandra P. Aldrich, and I have met or who sent letters to me. Some of the people felt hopeless; some were about to commit suicide. Others were tempted to run away from their families and responsibilities. Some were behind a mahogany desk; others behind bars.

Perhaps you haven't been behind bars, but you may be in a situation where you have lost freedom. Perhaps you haven't had a crisis pregnancy, but you may have a crisis in which you are thinking, *This can't be happening to me now.* I hope you've never thought suicide was your only way out as the young mother in one of the narratives thought, but you may be wondering, *Where do I turn next?* The answer, of course, is to Scripture.

Plan a time to regularly read through this book. Perhaps reading a chapter a day, including the Scripture that impacted the people's lives, will help you develop the routine of reading the Bible every day. At the back of the book you will find a summary listing of the Scriptures to ponder for each story. Use this section as a "21 Day Bible Reading Plan." It is a simple, easy way to add Bible reading to your daily routine, to dip into some of the highlights of Scripture without feeling you have to read through the entire Bible this year. Before you know it, you will want to read more. In fact, why not next try the "90 Days to Wisdom and Praise" Bible reading plan, which is intended for people who after 21 days say, "I want more! Is that all there is?" At the back of the book, you will find a fresh new Bible reading plan that will help you capture the story of God in the Bible over a three-month period. The goal simply is to help you with your personal spiritual discipline of Bible reading. My prayer is that the time you designate regularly for Bible reading will help energize your spiritual life and love of Scripture and provide rewarding encounters with the living Christ. The next thing you know, you might find yourself reading through the entire Bible, perhaps for the first time ever.

Sandra and I have changed the identities of most of the twenty-one people who have shared their stories and have given them only a first name. If both first and last names are listed, you may be assured that is the person's true identity. Many of these people are still in the process of becoming followers of Christ, so you may want to join us in praying for the continuing impact of the Word of God in their lives.

We have also added To Ponder questions at the end of each story along with suggestions for Scripture that might help you make a personal connection between God's Word and your own challenges. In this book you will read stories about people who were far from God and encountered him in the Bible. Many took Christ as their Lord and Savior. You will also find ministry leaders who are close to God and have encountered God's direction and will for their lives through the pages of the Bible. These are called "Encounter Stories." The end result in both stories and encounters is lives changed for eternity as people encounter God in the Bible.

So, come along and enjoy these stories of lives changed as they encounter the living God through the pages of his Word. And may this encourage you to connect with that same power for your life as well. Our prayer is that you will be encouraged to read God's Word even more and to sensitively and effectively share it with others who need to make their own connection.

Thomas L. Youngblood
Colorado Springs, Colorado

1Beauty from Ashes

Oh, the depth of the riches of the wisdom and knowledge of God! How unsearchable his judgments, and his paths beyond tracing out!

Romans 11:33

Early on the morning of September 11, 2001, Tom McGuinness kissed his wife, Cheryl, goodbye and left for Boston's Logan airport, where he was scheduled to copilot American Airlines Flight 11 to Los Angeles.

After driving their children, sixteen-year-old Jennifer and fourteen-year-old Tommy, to school, Cheryl poured a cup of coffee, grabbed a quilt and her Bible, and sat on the back porch of their Portsmouth, New Hampshire, home. Just as she finished praying, the phone rang. It was a friend, asking if Tom was home. At her negative answer, he hesitantly told her a plane had been hijacked, and that he and his wife were on their way over to stay with her until they knew Tom was all right.

Cheryl grabbed the TV remote, but none of the buttons seemed to work. Then Jennifer and Tommy called, having heard the report at school, wondering if their dad was okay. The house quickly filled with friends who prayed with Cheryl as they waited. She was frustrated, then frantic at the lack of news. Then Boston's chief pilot for American Airlines arrived and sadly gave her the official word: Flight 11 had not only been hijacked but had been deliberately flown into New York City's World Trade Center.

Cheryl reeled, hysterical. "No, God, please don't call him home," she sobbed.

Friends drove Cheryl to school, where she met Jennifer and Tommy in the principal's office. They knew from the look on their mother's face she had bad news. All she could utter was, "Jesus called Daddy home."

They hugged and cried as Cheryl said God would take care of all of them, but they knew their lives had been changed forever.

In the days that followed, Cheryl felt broken beyond what could ever be repaired. And the woman who had once described herself as a control freak was anything but in control. She was now totally dependent upon God and often began her prayers with "I can't go on alone. You are the only one who can get me through this."

Tom's memorial service was a tribute to his faith as hundreds packed their church, dabbing at their eyes as Tommy described how his father read the Bible each morning, providing memory stacked upon memory of his faithfulness to God's Word. Cheryl hugged that scene to herself, thankful

Jennifer and Tommy had had a godly dad and had observed a loving husband's faith in action. But the days following the service were filled with constant reminders of her grief. Even during quick trips to the grocery store, she seemed to see only couples walking hand in hand.

And, of course, she grappled with the toughest of all questions: *Why did this happen?* All of America had been struggling with this issue, but for Cheryl the question was personal as she wondered, *Why Tom?* Then, *Why me? And what about our precious children? Who will walk Jen down the aisle some day? Who will teach Tommy to shave?*

Her only comfort came as she looked to God's Word and found assurance after assurance that her heavenly Father was with them all.

She tried to maintain a regular home routine for the sake of the children as well as her own emotional stability. But during those early days, she felt all she could do was read the Word and pray. Her prayers were mostly cries for the Lord to hold her, comfort her, and strengthen her in her new roles as widow and single mom.

"I would groan to God on my knees, knowing he hears my prayers," Cheryl says. "Isaiah 65:24 proclaims, 'Before they call I will answer; while they are still speaking I will hear.' I still take special comfort in that."

She also thanks God for protecting her from knowing the future. The last night with Tom was a special evening as they celebrated his forty-second birthday. After a two-day trip he had come home to a delicious meal Cheryl had taken all day to prepare. Jennifer's present to her dad was a love certificate for the two of them to go out to an Italian restaurant. Tommy's gift was to spend time with him working in the backyard for a day of cleaning up the woods.

That night, Cheryl told Tom how she had seen God shape and mold him, and how honored she felt to be his wife. As she again said, "I love you," his eyes shone, knowing the depth of her expression.

As she replayed that evening in her mind, she was grateful God had not told her what the next morning would bring. If she had known, she is convinced she would have spent their final hours together pleading with God not to call Tom home.

"Our last night would have been very different," she says. "Realizing this helps me accept that God knows the times and seasons in our lives, and I don't need to know everything. In fact, I shouldn't know everything. I just need to move forward, trusting God each step of the way.

"I've experienced the truth of the first part of Psalm 145:20 and I'm trusting him for the second part," she says. 'The Lord watches over all who love him, but all the wicked he will destroy.'

"We live in a world in which evil seems to progress unchecked," she says. "When freedom is exercised in defiance of God, there are terrible consequences. In the blink of an eye, Tom and many others were killed. But God invites us to use our freedom to honor him. God is the only way I can survive. I'm comforted knowing the Lord cradled Tom in his arms as the plane hit the World Trade Center and then he carried him home. Our heavenly Father was there when his Son was hung on a cross and crucified; he was there when Tom's plane crashed. And I am convinced Jesus wept with me and with the others who hurt. Knowing that, my personal relationship with the Lord will never be the same. He cares about my pain and he will settle my heart if I trust him."

Cheryl is experiencing a deep connection to numerous friends, old and new, across the nation as people have reached out with love and tenderness. Further, she often is encouraged by her children.

Recently, Jennifer said, "Mom, I'm so glad you're not angry at God."

"I'm glad you're not angry either," Cheryl responded.

Jennifer nodded. "I know God didn't cause this to happen," she said. "God is getting me through this."

Another night, Tommy put his arm around Cheryl's shoulders as she cried, and said, "Mom, our life on earth is so short. Our life in heaven with Dad is for eternity." Then he added, "Dad described eternity this way to me, 'If you emptied all the oceans in the world one drop at a time, this would only be the beginning of eternity.'"

Cheryl says that in addition to encouragement, God has renewed her purpose.

"He is bringing me from confusion to clarity," she says. "I'm learning new ways to trust him and not lean on my own understanding—just as Proverbs 3:4–6 commands. This ordeal has been devastating, and I can't begin to figure it out, but I trust God has good things in store for us."

She continues, "1 Corinthians 2:9 says, 'No eye has seen, no ear has heard, no mind has conceived what God has prepared for those who love him.' I do love God with all my heart—as did Tom. The Lord gave Tom his reward early—eternal life. Of course, it came earlier than I would have liked, but God is in control, not I.

"If I doubt that, all I have to do is look to Isaiah 55:8, which reminds me God's ways are not our ways. If I lived my way, I certainly would do things differently. But I don't live my way. I live in obedience to my Lord even when it doesn't feel good. I never thought this time of being left alone would come so soon, but I know God is in control, and he loves me more than I can comprehend."

While Cheryl always loved the Scriptures, they now have come alive to her.

"I cling to every promise," she says. "To trust in the Word of God is hard sometimes, yet at the same time it brings incredible peace. A few weeks before Tom died, he told me to trust in God if anything ever happened. Something did. And it was terrible. But I am trusting God, and finding that he truly is trustworthy."

TO PONDER
- Have you ever lost someone through a tragic death?
- What helped you the most?
- In what areas are you still hurting?
- What suggestions do you have for those who want to help others?

MAKE A PERSONAL CONNECTION ON DAY 1

The crucifixion of Jesus: John 19:17–37
Scripture fulfilled: Psalm 22:18

ENCOUNTER STORY

For your Maker is your husband—the Lord Almighty is his name—the Holy One of Israel is your Redeemer; he is called the God of all the earth.

Isaiah 54:5

When my thirty-nine-year-old husband, Don, died of brain cancer, I felt lost. How was I, a Kentucky woman who had been trained "to take care of a man and youngins and have a big garden and quilt" going to raise two children alone? The worries seemed greater in the evenings, so after I put our ten-year-old son, Jay, and eight-year-old daughter, Holly, to bed, I couldn't stand the thought of going back downstairs. In the past, after the kids were asleep, Don and I talked about the day's challenges, then we would dream about a better future. Often we'd build a fire and sip mugs of spiced tea as we talked about our little ones. We had even planned which colleges they'd go to. Suddenly I was facing those future days alone.

So each evening, I would tuck both children in bed, pray with them, and then go to my own lonely bedroom. There propped up in bed and with a quilt around my shoulders, I would read every grief book I could get my hands on—all the way from clinical reports from experts to the down-home experiences of other widows. But nothing eased the knot around my heart.

It was only when I set aside all the books and picked up the Bible that healing began. As I read Jeremiah 10:19 in the King James Version—"This is a grief and I must bear it"—I thought of my grandmother saying, "Honey, there are some things in life that all you can do with them is bear them." But I realized I could not bear this grief alone. From Jeremiah, I turned to Philippians 4:19—"But my God shall supply all your need according to his riches in glory by Christ Jesus." Then I read Isaiah 54:5—"For thy maker is thy husband, the Lord Almighty is his name."

In the days ahead, that verse would help me make scary decisions. When I was offered a career change three years later that meant a move to New York, I started to panic over where we would live and where Jay and Holly would go to school. One night, I could not get to sleep until I finally said aloud, "Lord, husbands worry about housing and schooling. You're my husband, you figure it out, I'm going to sleep."

Letting go of worry over my responsibilities helped me have the best night's sleep I'd had in a long time. Oh, there were still plenty of rough days ahead, but I was learning to trust my husband of the Scriptures. To trust him not only with my eternal life, but with my day-to-day decision making. And none of that would have come if I'd still been trying to glean strength from the grief experts.

Sandra P. Aldrich, President and CEO
Bold Words, Inc.
Colorado Springs, Colorado

2 Bible in Camouflage

But we prayed to our God and posted a guard day and night to meet this threat.

Nehemiah 4:9

Philip lowered his head to pass under the door frame of the mud-walled house and then stepped into the morning's freezing rain, his hand tightening on his semiautomatic rifle. Back home, the Green Mountains would be filled with the colors of autumn—especially the orange and red maples on his parents' farm. Each October, no matter where he was in the world, his thoughts turned to New England. But he'd been in the Army's Special Forces—commonly known as the Green Berets—for so long that he hadn't seen his mountains in full color for several years.

"This sure is a long way from Vermont," he muttered to no one in particular as he looked toward the barren folds of mountains that had hidden the Taliban soldiers just the week before. After the September 11 attacks on the United States,

Philip knew his team would be one of the first ones sent in since he and the five men with whom he served were trained for special duty in the Middle East, including being fluent in Arabic.

Since their arrival three weeks ago, he and his team had directed wave after wave of American planes against Taliban targets in Northern Afghanistan. Even though they wore long hair and beards to blend into the local population, their height and semiautomatic weapons quickly marked them as Americans.

The team's first hurdle had been to gain the confidence of the Afghan commanders of the Northern Alliance. Part of the problem was the Afghans' skepticism that American planes could hit a precise target—namely the Taliban troops—without killing nearby Northern Alliance soldiers. After lengthy discussions that often included detailed explanations of modern weaponry, Philip and the others finally were driven to a hill overlooking the Taliban lines. There, they set up their equipment, including telescopes, laser-range finders, target designators, and two-way radios. At their call, a B–52 flying more than three miles high dropped 2,000-pound bombs that landed perfectly. The Americans now had the total confidence of the Northern Alliance commanders.

For the next several weeks, Philip's team made daily treks to the nearby frontlines in a shaky borrowed truck until a C–130 transport could deliver a new all-terrain vehicle. From their positions, the team sighted the target, then directed airstrikes all day long—and occasionally into the night. Often those calls put their own lives in danger, and they had to flatten themselves in shallow trenches and cover their heads from exploding rocks. But hour after hour, the airstrikes destroyed the Taliban defenses. Finally, the Taliban had little choice but to surrender.

Now as he stepped into the cold morning, Philip patted his pocket to make sure his Bible was there. He and his team had been warned the mission would be extremely dangerous and all had been reminded—unnecessarily—to have their affairs in order. After all, the area had been filled with several nationalities of extremists who stated they would fight to the death.

At 31, Philip was the "old man" on the team and had seen more than his share of tough times. But he still carried the Bible with the sand camouflage cover he had received from a chaplain as his company of "kids," as he now calls them, awaited orders in December 1990. The Gulf War was over just as it was getting started, but Philip had reconnected with the faith of his childhood through that little book and continued to read its pages every chance he got—for reassurance as well as moral direction.

Even though the bombing had been halted, Philip and his men stayed in the area to assist the new local government, even repairing generators to provide the first electricity since the Taliban rule. Furthermore, the team arranged numerous nighttime airdrops of food and blankets for the Afghans.

Philip's quick smile as he hands food to a child emphasizes his pleasure that he's no longer calling in planes but can concentrate more on humanitarian aid. He will never forget the moment when he heard a child laugh and realized that the entire group of people standing nearby had turned at the sound. Most of them had not heard the forbidden laughter during the entire reign of the Taliban. But that was also a moment of fear for the people since many Taliban sympathizers are still in the region. Because of that presence, Philip and his team continue to take seriously guard duty and defensive planning.

It still will be a long time before he gets back to his Vermont mountains.

TO PONDER

- Have you or someone you love ever been in combat? What was the situation?
- What helped?
- What types of non-military battles have you experienced?
- What did you need then?

MAKE A PERSONAL CONNECTION ON DAY 2

David meets Goliath: 1 Samuel 17:32–50
Rebuilding the wall: Nehemiah 4:14–20

ENCOUNTER STORY

> *For I am the Lord, your God, who takes hold of your right hand and says to you, Do not fear; I will help you.*
>
> *Isaiah 41:13*

When I was the world leader of the Salvation Army, I faced an arduous challenge. In Russia, following Gorbachev's liberalization through *glasnost* and *perestroika,* I was faced with the challenge as to whether the Salvation Army should return to Russia. We had been banned by the Communist authorities almost seventy years before. But with Communism becoming discredited, and the people in a state of uncertainty, was this an open door for us to return? But there were many difficulties. We no longer had any Salvationists in Russia, we were unknown there, and the financial resources needed would be phenomenal. Could we hope to tackle such a herculean task?

During this decisive time, I was visiting the United States and was struck by a headline in the newspaper *USA Today.* Surprisingly, it was in Latin—*Carpe Diem*—which means *Seize the day.* Grasp the opportunity. That seemed like a message for me, but I needed confirmation from God's Word. At the time, I was reading from the book of the prophet Isaiah, and that morning's passage read, "For I am the Lord, your God, who takes hold of your right hand and says to you, Do not fear, I will help you."

That was the word I needed. His hand would guide me. Why should I fear? And his hand did guide. We returned to Russia, millions of dollars came in from even the most unexpected sources, and people from all around the world volunteered.

Yes, we went in. The door opened. Russians opened their hearts to the gospel. And the Salvation Army has never looked back.

Eva Burrows, General (Ret)
Salvation Army
Melbourne, Australia

ENCOUNTER STORY

> *After I looked things over, I stood up and said to the nobles, the officials and the rest of the people, "Don't be afraid of them. Remember the Lord, who is great and awesome, and fight for your brothers, your sons and your daughters, your wives and your homes."*
>
> Nehemiah 4:14

"Be not afraid of them. Remember the Lord" is a portion of God's Word that has helped me maintain a godly focus and has given me courage in times of trouble and stress, both personally and in my ministry. The promise of the Lord's presence, strength, and protection has been real and sufficient for each trial. This clear and powerful reminder that Nehemiah gave to God's people in a time of crisis is not only practical but has comforted and encouraged me when the Enemy has attacked. The Lord is my strength and my all-sufficient Savior.

Dr. Gilbert A. Peterson, Chancellor
Lancaster Bible College
Lancaster, Pennsylvania

3 *An Early Morning Commute*

Do not be anxious about anything, but in everything, by prayer and petition, with thanksgiving, present your requests to God.

Philippians 4:6

Peter stood on the Metro North platform waiting for the 7:02 out of Mt. Kisco, New York. He would have a fifty-five-minute ride to Grand Central Station. From there he would be going to a meeting he was not looking forward to. The company was going to make changes, and he wasn't sure what those changes would be. All he knew was that the sky was gray, he was cold, and he did not want to be attending this meeting.

When the train arrived, he filed in with the rest of the passengers. As a veteran commuter, he knew to take a seat near the window so no one would have to climb over him as the train became more crowded with each stop. New Yorkers are accustomed to using travel time to read or sort through files from their briefcases. But Peter stared grumpily out the window, paying no attention as those from the next stops at Chappaqua and Pleasantville got on, and the seat next to him became occupied. Still forty minutes to go. He pondered the meeting. What would he say?

He was momentarily distracted by the armless man across the aisle who nonchalantly handed his ticket to the conductor after pulling it out of his suit jacket pocket with his toes, but Peter quickly overcame his surprise. Strange things were always happening in New York. He gave a little huff, thinking about the meeting he was dreading. Well, worrying about it wasn't going to help, so he opened his briefcase and pulled out the New Testament he always carried with him. He turned to the encouragement of Matthew 10:18–20:

> On my account, you will be brought before governors and kings as witnesses to them and to the Gentiles. But when they arrest you, do not worry about what to say or how to say it. At that time, you will be given what to say, for it will not be you speaking, but the Spirit of your Father speaking through you.

Well, he certainly wasn't planning on being arrested, but it was nice to know he didn't have to worry about what to say. As he pondered the reminder that he wasn't going into the meeting alone, the passenger next to him suddenly spoke.

"Are you reading the Koran?" the man asked.

"No, I'm reading God's truth, the New Testament," Peter replied, surprised to hear a fellow commuter actually talking.

"How interesting," the man replied. "I read the Koran each morning before I leave my home. I've noticed my day goes better if I start with it."

Peter closed his Bible and held it out to the young Muslim. "Would you like to have this copy to compare to the Koran?" he asked.

The man paused for only a moment. "Yes, thank you. I would like that very much," he said. "Where was it you were reading?"

Peter opened to Matthew 10, but said, "You might like to start reading at chapter one. It begins with the genealogy from Abraham and then goes into the birth of Jesus."

The young man carefully turned the thin pages to the beginning of Matthew and began reading.

Peter smiled. *Why am I worrying about the meeting? It's going to be a piece of cake.* And he settled against the window.

TO PONDER

- Are you comfortable reading the Bible in public? Why or why not?
- If so, have you ever been asked what you were reading?
- Would you be comfortable giving your Bible to a stranger?

MAKE A PERSONAL CONNECTION ON DAY 3

A weak man made strong: Judges 6:12–7:9
Jesus fills the nets: John 21:1–14

ENCOUNTER STORY

> *The weapons we fight with are not the weapons of the world.
> On the contrary, they have divine power to demolish strong-
> holds. We demolish arguments and every pretension that sets
> itself up against the knowledge of God, and we take captive
> every thought to make it obedient to Christ.*
>
> *2 Corinthians 10:4–5*

During my early twenties, by God's "severe mercy," I was bumping into just about every possible intellectual challenge to my faith—from people in cults, world religions, and various strains of religious liberalism and skepticism. I had grown up in a Christian home and a Bible-teaching congregation, but I soon realized the words of the song we sang in church, "You ask me how I know he lives? He lives within my heart," though true, fell woefully short in helping me shore up my own faith, much less spread it to others.

During that time I stumbled upon the Scripture in 2 Corinthians 10:4–5 that changed my perspective as I realized the weapons we fight with are not the weapons of the world. On the contrary, they have divine power to demolish stronghold. We demolish arguments and every pretension that sets itself up against the knowledge of God, and we take captive every thought to make it obedient to Christ.

These verses filled me with boldness, giving me a new attitude concerning what I believed. I didn't need to be defensive *about* my faith. I needed to get on the offense *with* it! Truth, logic, evidence, spiritual power—these are ours in Christ, and we need to act as though we possess them, humbly and gently but confidently communicating Christianity to the people around us.

I found, both then and now, that when I do this, another verse proves true as well. It's Romans 1:16, which assures us that we need not be ashamed of the gospel, "because it is the power of God for the salvation of everyone who believes."

Mark Mittelberg, Evangelism Champion and Author
Willow Creek Association
South Barrington, Illinois

ENCOUNTER STORY

I am the vine; you are the branches. If a man remains in me and I in him, he will bear much fruit; apart from me you can do nothing.

John 15:5

When stepping into full-time ministry more than five years ago, those words of Jesus from John 15:5 served as a reminder to me to stay connected to the Source. Today, they continue to remind me that on my own, I can do nothing. Staying connected means daily time in the Word, in prayer, and in fellowship with other Christians.

Rich Blanco, Outreach Director
International Bible Society
Colorado Springs, Colorado

4 One Lonely Soul

*Though you have not seen him, you love him; and even though
you do not see him now, you believe in him and are filled with
an inexpressible and glorious joy.*

1 Peter 1:8

Twenty-two-year-old Marissa felt more like eighty as she
eased her nine-month-old daughter, Jenny, into her crib, then
paused to make sure the settling against the mattress hadn't
awakened her. She caressed the baby's soft cheek before
turning toward the single bed where three-year-old Brianna
slept. Normally, she couldn't get both of them settled into
bed until almost midnight. But here it was only 9:30, and
already they were asleep. She pulled the blanket up around
her daughter's shoulders, marveling at her quiet breathing,
her sweet silence. All day long, day in and day out, she displayed boundless energy—jumping, running, yelling, whin-
ing—while Marissa sat on the sofa, holding the baby and
watching. Most days that's all Marissa had the energy to do—

watch. In fact, usually she could just barely prepare bottles for the baby and get simple meals for Brianna and herself. How could she feel so very old so very soon?

This wasn't the life she had planned—for herself or her children. But she had listened to too many meaningless promises and now she was stuck in a world she hadn't signed on for—that of a single welfare mother. Her daughters deserved so much more than her weariness. She ought to be taking them to the park each afternoon. She ought to be making cookies with Brianna. But she was just so tired. If only she had a girlfriend or a kind neighbor who would give her a break now and again. But it was only her. Her children deserved two parents who would love them and play with them and help them find their own way in this world.

Marissa sighed as she turned toward the bedroom door. Well, maybe she could give them that new life now. She'd found a street source of sleeping pills and had saved thirty-eight pills. That ought to do the job right. The pills wouldn't be messy, and Brianna wouldn't be scared. The police would come; then they'd call the social services lady, who would find a nice home for the children. Jenny would adjust right away since she was so young, and Brianna would quickly forget once she got settled in a new place. A slight smile settled around the corners of Marissa's lips as she nodded at mental scenes of both little girls clad in matching pajamas as they snuggled against their new parents.

But what if they're not placed in the same home? she thought in horror. *They've got to grow up together!*

She'd have to leave a note to tell the authorities where she wanted the children placed. Maybe even suggest that nice woman and her husband she had worked with a couple of years ago. And, of course, she needed to tell the new parents Brianna likes teddy bears. That would help them win her over quickly.

Marissa glanced at the small notepad by the phone. No, ordinary paper wouldn't do. She needed something pretty—like the box of stationery someone had given her several birthdays ago. She had thought it was too pretty to use, so she had kept it unopened—until now.

She opened her closet door, then pulled the light chain, momentarily squinting in the sudden brightness. What a mess! How long had it been since she had cleaned this out? What was it she was looking for again? She began to pull items aimlessly off the shelves, then stood on tiptoe to pull others onto the floor—a murder mystery, a book of baby names, a sewing kit, a fabric-covered stationery box, a small blue book. Suddenly the title of the blue book caught her attention—*Hope for the Future.*

Startled by the title, she slid to the floor and thumbed through the thin pages.

Hope. Now that's something I can use right now, she thought. *Where'd I get this? Oh, yeah. Somebody gave it to me when I was pregnant with Brianna.*

Turning the book toward the light, she began with the section "How to find peace." John 16:33 almost seemed to glow as she read, "I have told you these things, so that in me you may have peace. In this world you will have trouble. But take heart! I have overcome the world."

This is a Bible! she thought. Eagerly she turned page after page, unaware of how long she sat on the closet floor as new strength pushed through her weariness. As she turned to the final pages, she read again of the love that had caused Jesus to willingly accept crucifixion. Tears formed in her eyes as she read, "You can begin a personal relationship with God by simply telling him that you believe. You can use your own words, or these:

> *Dear God, I know that my sin has separated me from you, and I admit my sin. I'm sorry. I know you love me and that you sent Jesus to die on the cross, in my place, taking the penalty for my sin. Thank you. I want to turn from my sin and begin to follow and serve you. I give myself to you. Please begin to direct my life. Thank you for giving me new life. In Jesus' name I pray. Amen.*

Marissa pulled herself to her knees, clasped her hands tightly, and read the words again—this time aloud—as tears ran down her cheeks. At her whispered *amen,* she stretched out on the floor, sobbing out years of anguish. Finally, she lay very still, marveling at the quiet strength that surged through her limbs. Suddenly she sat up.

What had the book said about telling five people about this new life? she wondered.

"God, I don't have *five* people to tell," she whispered.

The answer was almost audible: *Then write a letter.*

The fabric-covered stationery box was on the floor next to her. Eagerly, she checked the front pages of the Bible for the publisher's address: *International Bible Society, Colorado Springs, Colorado.* She jumped to her feet, grabbed a pen from the nightstand, and smiled as she pulled a sheet of paper from the box.

Dear International Bible Society,

I'm not sure how to begin this letter, so I will just go with the flow. First I want to say thank you. I'm 22 years old and for so long I have felt dead. . . .

Her new life had begun.

TO PONDER

- If you have ever identified with any part of Marissa's situation, what encouraged you?
- How do you react to Marissa not having five people to tell?

MAKE A PERSONAL CONNECTION ON DAY 4

Hagar and her son, Ishmael: Genesis 21:8–21
The birth of Jesus: Matthew 1:18–24

ENCOUNTER STORY

You did not choose me, but I chose you and appointed you to go and bear fruit—fruit that will last. Then the Father will give you whatever you ask in my name.

John 15:16

This is the verse God used to call me to the ministry of MOPS International, a ministry of lifestyle evangelism to mothers. Truly, when a mom enters into a saving relationship with Jesus Christ, she finds a hope beyond herself. God never meant for us to mother alone. He wants to touch our children through us. A mom bears fruit that will last when she finds Jesus and passes her faith on to her children—and her world.

Elisa Morgan, President
MOPS International (Mothers of Preschoolers)
Denver, Colorado

ENCOUNTER STORY

> *Fear not, for I have redeemed you; I have called you by name;*
> *you are mine. When you pass through the waters, I will be with*
> *you; and when you pass through the rivers, they will not sweep*
> *over you. When you walk through the fire, you will not be*
> *burned; the flames will not set you ablaze. For I am the Lord*
> *your God, the Holy One of Israel, your Savior.*
>
> *Isaiah 43:1–3*

When a Bible passage speaks to me as I'm reading, I jot the date in the margin. It's interesting to review those specific verses, especially when I've put several dates next to them. Isaiah 43:1b–3a is such a verse.

When my husband, Bill, died, and I was searching for encouragement as to how I would manage alone and raise two young children, that verse was one of several that were just for me. When I thought I was in danger of losing my job, when I faced a major move, and when I later started my own consulting business, God always brought me back to this portion of his Word. It doesn't say, "I will make it go away." But it does say he will get me through it. I can't avoid the pain, but I have a God who will get me through to the other side."

Bobbie Valentine, President and CEO
Bobbie Valentine Media Consulting, Inc.
Glendora, California

5 In the Beginning

In the beginning God created the heavens and the earth. Now the earth was formless and empty, darkness was over the surface of the deep, and the Spirit of God was hovering over the waters.

Genesis 1:1–2

Carlos stood before the open door of his newly assigned cell. Finally the guard muttered, "Might as well go in and get used to it. You're going to be here awhile."

As Carlos took a deep breath and stepped forward, the guard pulled the barred door shut. For a long moment, Carlos stood in the dim light looking at the place that would be his home for the next eight to ten years.

The single cot was covered with a coarse gray blanket. A stainless steel sink and commode were in one corner. A small metal stand was at the end of the bed. The two drawers would hold the few personal items he was allowed.

Carlos pulled open the top drawer and discovered a tattered Bible. Since he couldn't read well, he picked it up merely out of curiosity and thumbed through the pages, staring at the chapter headings without recognition. Then he thrust the Scriptures back into the drawer, sank onto his cot, and buried his face in his hands.

The days that followed were filled with early rising, supervised showers, and rotated times for shaving with a communal electric shaver. He missed the close shaves he had been able to get with his safety razor at home, but that was before his wrong choices had thrust him into this place.

After breakfast, some of the men on his cell block took court-ordered anger management classes, others worked out in the weight room. Carlos moved from one painful memory to another. The waiting was broken only by mealtimes, and he tried not to think how many endless days are in eight to ten years.

One night, several weeks after his arrival, Carlos realized the next day would be his wedding anniversary.

Ten years, he thought. *I had so many plans back then.*

He remembered how his wife's eyes had shone as she repeated her vows. *Rose deserves so much more than what she got from me,* he thought. *Will she wait for a loser? Our little boys need a daddy. They'll be teens before I get out.*

As he thought about his children growing up without their father just as he had grown up without his, pain curled around his heart. Crying was not something he wanted to do, but within his mind, he bellowed, "God, if you are real, you've got to help me."

In the quiet moments that followed, an idea settled into his mind: *Get that old Bible and start at the beginning.*

He shook off the command. *Why bother? I can't read.*

The thought persisted, though. Finally, Carlos stood up, numbly thinking that maybe just holding the Bible would offer comfort. He opened the drawer, pulled out the volume, and opened to what he later would discover was Genesis 1:1.

In addition to simple words such as *and* or *the,* Carlos knew the word *God.* So he went through the first chapter and counted the number of times he saw *God.* As he looked at the unfamiliar words, he ran his fingers over the print—as though wishing the meanings would enter through his touch.

The next morning, in the dayroom, he saw one of his cell block neighbors writing a letter.

"Where'd you get the paper?" Carlos asked.

The man didn't look up. "The chaplain."

Back at his cell with a newly acquired paper and pen, Carlos laboriously printed the words *beginning* and *created,* then folded the paper so it would fit in the palm of his hand. On their way to lunch, Carlos showed the paper to the man who had been writing the letter earlier.

"What are these words?" he asked quietly, afraid the man would ridicule him. But the other prisoner merely glanced at the paper and replied just as quietly, "The first word is *beginning;* the other is *created.* Why?"

"No reason," Carlos replied. "Just wondering. Thanks."

Back in his cell, Carlos looked at the verse again and slowly mouthed, "In the beginning God created."

Surges of excitement and hope ran through him, and he read the words again: "In the beginning God created."

Those five words were the start of an incredible journey for Carlos as each day he wrote two or three more words on his paper and showed it to inmates he knew could read. It took him eight days to get through the 31 verses of chapter one. In the weeks that followed, he not only learned to read, but he discovered a hunger for what God might create in his own life.

Today, after serving six years of his sentence—with time off for good behavior—Carlos has earned his GED diploma and graduated from his local Bible school. Not only does he share his story readily, but as an ordained minister he pastors, with the help of his wife, Rose, a small church filled with other folks who need the hope of those long ago words: "In the beginning God created."

TO PONDER

- Have you ever felt totally hopeless? What was the situation?
- Did you find encouragement?
- If so, what helped?
- If not, what did you need?

MAKE A PERSONAL CONNECTION ON DAY 5

The creation: Genesis 1:1–31
One of Paul's prison letters: 2 Timothy 1:1–12

ENCOUNTER STORY

*May your ways be known on earth, your salvation among all
nations.*

Psalms 67:2

Psalm 67:2 is my life verse. Since I was called out of physical medicine into spiritual medicine, the greatest joy and fulfillment in my life comes when a person receives Jesus Christ as Lord and Savior.

The second greatest sounding note is struck when that person takes the ways of God, as shown in his Word, and becomes part of changing society, beginning with self as an individual, then his or her family and, finally, the corporate society in which he or she lives.

Our Lord wants salvation known throughout the earth and his ways known by everyone possible. Certainly, there will be tares among the wheat and brands to be plucked from the burning when that trumpet ending this age sounds, heralding the Lord's coming. The practical answer given by our Lord regarding the question "What about those who never hear?" is the Great Commission. Our job is to leave the answer to that question to the Lord and, while we await his coming, tell the Good News to individuals, help them respond to the call of Christ, and then be a part of their discipleship throughout the world.

Nothing is more important than eternal values, and no value is more important than eternal life. Therefore, as Psalm 67:2 says, the driving force behind my service to the Lord is my desire to make his ways known. I trust he will take the service I render and accomplish his salvation through this inadequate vessel.

Tom Phillips, Vice President
Billy Graham Evangelistic Association
Asheville, North Carolina

6 A Life-Changing Match

*I have fought the good fight, I have finished the race, I have
kept the faith.*

2 Timothy 4:7

Dave pushed the locker room door shut with his tennis
racket. He'd lost the match, and the team had been counting
on him. If they had won this tournament, they would have
gone on to state. But he'd missed returning that last ball and
it had cost them the championship. And what aggravated
him the most was that he could have cheated and called the
ball out of bounds. It had been so close to the line his
opponent couldn't see it clearly. But, instinctively, Dave had
called it *in* and had handed the victory to the opponent.

What a dummy I am, he thought. *Who cares whether
or not anybody lies over the call of the ball?*

Dave couldn't wait to get to his car. He wanted out of
this building and out of these tormenting thoughts.

Just as he arrived at his vehicle, he heard his name
called. He turned and saw Coach Aldrich hurrying to him.

When Coach arrived, he put his arm around Dave's shoulder. "I was at the doubles court during your last set," he said. "I didn't see the final volley, but I heard about it."

Dave cringed, but Coach continued. "I just wanted you to know I'm proud of you. A lesser man would have lied and called the ball out. The other coach was standing behind you and saw how close it was. You've got to know, he's really impressed with your caliber."

Dave muttered, "Yeah, thanks, but it cost us the tournament."

Coach nodded. "I know," he said. "But in the great scheme of things, it's your honesty that's going to matter, not the tournament. We have to look at ourselves every day in the mirror, and those seemingly little decisions start us on major pathways. You did the right thing, son. I'm proud of you."

Then Coach thumped Dave's shoulder. "Now don't forget; everybody's meeting at my house at 6:30. Come hungry."

It crossed Dave's mind not to go, but he figured if Coach made that much of an effort to encourage him, he ought to be there. At least he wouldn't let any of the other guys razz him about the call. The coach was always stressing honesty.

Sometimes I wonder what makes that guy tick, Dave thought.

At 6:30, the whole team was in Coach Aldrich's family room, guzzling colas and trying not to drop cheese on the carpet. Coach's wife kept bringing in platters of hot pizza and platefuls of her famous black walnut brownies. Their two little kids knew all of the players by name and were trying out their latest "Knock-Knock" jokes. Finally, the coach pulled his four-year-old daughter onto his lap and cleared his throat.

"Well, gang, we had a good year," he said. "Sure, we didn't make it as far as we hoped, but we got a lot farther than a lot of people thought we would."

He opened the shopping bag at his feet. "You need to know I'm proud of each one of you," he said. "You've grown this year, and I'm looking forward to watching where life takes you. To close out the season, I have a gift for you."

He reached into the bag and pulled out a New Testament. "This book contains principles that help me as I try to be a good husband and father as well as a good coach," he said as he handed the books, one by one, to his six-year-old son to give to each player. "I hope you'll remember what I've written in the front: 'Love in tennis means nothing. The love in this book means everything.' If you remember that, you'll have an easier time with all of life's matches."

Dave looked at the copy in his hands. *So this is what makes Coach tick,* he thought. And he knew he would be reading it often in the days ahead.

TO PONDER

- Have you ever had to make a call in a sports event that made the difference in the game? If so, what was the situation?
- Do you agree with the saying, "It's not the winning or losing that's important, but how you play the game"? Why or why not?
- What advice do you have for young athletes?

MAKE A PERSONAL CONNECTION ON DAY 6

The burning bush: Exodus 3:1–14
Parable of the sower: Matthew 13:1–23

ENCOUNTER STORY

> *Whatever you do, work at it with all your heart, as working for the Lord, not for men.*
>
> *Colossians 3:23*

Toward the end of my junior year in college, Colossians 3:23 started to come alive to me. I realized that even my sports—soccer and baseball—should be done with a two-fold purpose: (1) with all my heart—every ounce of energy that I could muster for *training* as well as in games and (2) that I should play with all my heart *for God* and not for myself. God then started molding me for a life of "Sports Ministry." Now I'm able to combine the two things I am passionate about—leading people to Christ and competitive athletics.

Mark Steffens, Head Coach
Missionary Athletes International and Charlotte Eagles
Waxhaw, North Carolina

ENCOUNTER STORY

O Lord, you have searched me and you know me.

Psalm 139:1

Nearly thirty years ago, the study of the Gospel of John and the poignancy of Psalm 139 led me safely into the arms of my loving heavenly Father. The compelling reality of this intimate knowledge of my life (vv. 1–6), this powerful presence in my life (vv. 7–12), and this creative, unconditional love over my life (vv. 13–18), led me to invite him to become the Lord of my life. I regularly return to this psalm for comfort, counsel, and courage. It has dramatically influenced me as father, son, husband, brother, pastor, and friend.

Rev. Dr. Stephen A. Macchia, President
Vision New England
Acton, Massachusetts

7 A Counselor Needing a Counselor

And I will ask the Father, and he will give you another Counselor to be with you forever.

John 14:16

Sherry had a thriving counseling practice. In addition, she was tall and slim and carried herself with confidence. For all outward appearances, she was one who came to mind when people talked about others "having it all together." Her straight-shooting advice to couples—such as "don't expect others to meet all your needs" and "stop trying to fix the whole world"—and her practical suggestions for those wanting a new start in life were often quoted at coffee breaks. But her clients did not know about her own ongoing struggles.

As a child, she had been skinny, awkward, and shabbily dressed—an easy target for taunting classmates. Even after she had grown into a beautiful young woman with a counseling degree and fashionable wardrobe, she still thought of herself as unattractive and clumsy. That made her an easy target for flattering words from men who wanted more than friendship. But five years ago, when she had given birth out of wedlock to her son, Ethan, she set new goals as she stared into his tiny face. Thus, ignoring her own advice to others about not carrying inappropriate burdens, she determined to provide Ethan everything he would ever need. So she called on every ounce of her strength to cope with single parenthood while carrying a full counseling load. Then to add to the college fund she had started for him—he'd never have to work his way through school, she said—she took a part-time job as a night parent for children living in group-cottages since she could have Ethan with her. But once all the children had settled down, she felt lost and lonely. At home, she could ignore the feelings that threatened to swallow her by watching silly sitcoms on her wide screen TV. But the cottage contained only a static filled radio.

One night, she sprawled on the uncomfortable sofa where she slept.

What am I going to do with my life? she wondered. *Will I keep listening to the same stories from the same suburbanites? Why do I even bother to ask them for details? If they supply the names, I can tell them their own story.*

She rubbed her eyes. *But I've got to stay in the rat race if I'm going to send Ethan to the best schools. He's not going to struggle the way I did.*

Finally, she flung her arm over her eyes and whispered, "Well, God, if you aren't too busy, you are welcome to show up with your suggestions."

Fat chance of that, she thought as she stood up. *Well, find something boring to read and then go to sleep.*

She scanned the bookshelves that were filled with teen romance novels and comic books. A stack of outdated magazines filled the bottom shelf, topped with a couple of worn books that she discovered were New Testaments. She picked up the one entitled *Free on the Inside,* intrigued by the title. Soon she was reading through the Gospels just as though she were reading a gripping novel. Page after page seemed to speak directly to her frustration with life. She was especially taken with the accounts of Jesus withdrawing from the crowds to spend time with his heavenly Father.

He walked away from all those people to spend time in prayer, she pondered. *Even the Son of God needed recharging.*

Suddenly, she smiled. *In my practice, I've been working to change action, but the Bible is about changing attitude first. No wonder I've been so tired. I've gotta make some of my own changes—starting with finding ways to slow down.*

As she stared into the darkness, pondering that thought, she paused, then said aloud, "Hey, God, you did show up. Thanks!"

And with that assurance, she fell into the most restful sleep she'd had in weeks.

TO PONDER

- Have others ever considered you to be stronger than you actually are? If so, how did you react?
- Have you ever presented your weaknesses to the Lord? If so, what happened?

MAKE A PERSONAL CONNECTION ON DAY 7

Rich young man: Mark 10:17–29
God's counsel: Psalm 73:24

ENCOUNTER STORY

> *Train a child in the way he should go, and when he is old he will not turn from it.*
>
> *Proverbs 22:6*

> *Keep yourselves in God's love as you wait for the mercy of our Lord Jesus Christ to bring you to eternal life.*
>
> *Jude 21*

Proverbs 22:6 doesn't mean that all I have to do is realize what is best for my children, then bring them up with godly principles, and everything will be okay. Instead, it speaks to an awareness and appreciation of the individual bent of each child, which must be incorporated into parental instruction. Truly, God has made each one fearfully and wonderfully different.

That understanding not only has had an impact on my own family and on those in my family counseling practice, but on the millions who have heard my radio and TV commentaries or read my books.

I also appreciate Jude, verse 21, that implores us to stay within boundaries as we await our heavenly reward. What a great message for us all!

Dr. Kevin Leman, Radio Personality and Author
Real Families Ministry
Tucson, Arizona

ENCOUNTER STORY

Be still, and know that I am God.

Psalm 46:10

Perspective in life is often hard. Often, we are urged to action when we are not certain it is best. Sometimes we are frozen with fear, or confused by the din and roar of the moment. The hardest times for me, however, are not found in the midst of the battle; they are when I am alone with a tough decision. The very thought that through prayer and meditation, I have access to the wisest of counselors is a comfort, shield, and sword. After all, he is the one whose approval I seek with greatest fervor and the one who, as I seek him, will provide remarkable clarity in times of difficulty. To *be still* when I struggle and to *know* that God is in his heavens caring for me is a gift beyond my comprehension.

Andrew K. Benton, President
Pepperdine University
Malibu, California

8 *A Set Of Keys*

God is our refuge and strength, an ever-present help in trouble.
Psalm 46:1

Carolyn was barely in the intake room at the county jail when the officer handed her a piece of paper with a phone number on it.

"You're supposed to call this number right away," he said as he handed her a portable phone.

She stared at the number, recognizing it as her brother's.

Something bad has happened to the boys, she thought.

She stared at the phone for a long moment. If she didn't call, she wouldn't hear the news. Somehow in her mother's heart, she knew her sons were in trouble. Six and four years old, they were living with her brother while she awaited trial for burglary and possession of stolen goods. One stupid night of smoking weed had caused all this.

"Just one little job, and we've got enough to see us through the whole month, Sweets," her boyfriend had said.

Well, that one little job had already created one big mess. And now something bad was wrong with her boys.

"Lady, hurry and make the call," the officer said. "We gotta get you settled before quitting time."

She tried to keep her hands from shaking as she dialed. And she steeled herself for whatever she might hear. There was no way she was going to cry in front of these strangers.

For one glorious second, she was encouraged when her brother picked up the phone. Maybe everything was okay after all.

"Hey, this is Carolyn. What's up?"

As soon as she heard "Oh, Sis" she knew.

"What happened?" she begged.

"It's Darin, honey. Some guy went through a red light on us. Darin's side of the car was hit pretty bad. . . ." Her brother's voice broke.

"Is he. . . ? He's gonna be okay, though, right?"

"No. He didn't make it."

Screams were forming deep within her. She had to keep talking to keep them pushed down. "What about my other baby?"

"Paul's gonna be okay, but the hospital is keeping him overnight just to make sure." Then he added apologetically, "They released me already."

A long pause ensued as Carolyn struggled again to push the screams down. Finally her brother spoke again. "Look, I talked to the police chaplain there. He offered to tell you, but I told him I had to do this. He's planning to come by tomorrow morning to talk to you, though."

Another long pause came before he spoke again. "Sis, you need to know they aren't going to let you out to attend the funeral. I'm making the arrangements. We'll bury Darin next to Mama in Oak Grove. Is that okay?"

"Yeah, sure" was all she could manage before hanging up the phone. She had to keep those threatening screams under control.

She didn't remember being escorted to her cell, but suddenly there she was, sitting on the edge of the cell cot. She glanced around only once, then buried her face in her hands. How could her precious six-year-old be dead? He was always laughing at the silliest things. And he had just started school. He already had a sweet crush on his teacher. How could that child be dead?

And then the thought settled in—*he wouldn't be dead if you had been a decent mother and had been home with him.*

She clamped her hands over her mouth to muffle the sobs. Gradually, she realized someone was standing outside her cell. She hastily wiped her eyes and looked up. A tall, older woman stood there.

"You go right ahead and cry, honey" she said. "Bad news travels fast—especially in here. I know what happened. I'm sorry to hear it."

Carolyn nodded.

"Is there anything I can do for you?" the woman asked.

"Yeah. Do you have a set of keys?" Carolyn asked sarcastically.

The woman stepped closer to Carolyn's cell. "Yes, honey, I believe I do." And she pulled a small Bible out of her prison smock, thumbed through several pages, and held the open book to Carolyn.

"I thought you said you had keys," Carolyn snarled.

"Honey, the keys in here will open the most important door in the world, and that's the door to your heart. I had to learn that the hard way and, obviously, you will too. Here. You read right there—Matthew, chapter seven, verse seven—*Ask and it will be given to you; seek and you will find; knock and the door will be opened to you.* You're in a mess, and you need Jesus. He's the only one who's gonna be able to help you deal with this. But you got to ask for his help."

She continued to hold out the open Bible, until Carolyn—with tears streaming down her cheeks—stood up and gently took it from her hand.

TO PONDER

- Do you think this mother should have been allowed to attend her son's funeral? Why or why not?
- Have you ever been inside a jail? What were the circumstances?
- What do you think prisoners need most?

MAKE A PERSONAL CONNECTION ON DAY 8

Jesus and John the Baptist: Matthew 11:1–11
The early life of Moses: Exodus 2:1–15

ENCOUNTER STORY

> *Now to him who is able to do immeasurably more than all we ask or imagine, according to his power that is at work within us, to him be glory in the church and in Christ Jesus throughout all generations, for ever and ever! Amen.*
>
> *Ephesians 3:20–21*

God has powerfully impacted me with the realization that he is ferociously determined to fill the earth with his glory—through the church! (See Hebrews 2:14.) What amazes me about this is that God's glory is made known through fallible human beings.

"How can this be?" I asked the Lord many times. God's *glory* revealed through sinful saints?

"But that tells you what kind of God I am," the Lord assures me.

And what kind of glory? The glory of his mercy. Wow.

Floyd McClung, Senior Pastor
Metro Christian Fellowship
Kansas City, Kansas

9 God's Tattoos

So the other disciples told him, "We have seen the Lord!" But he said to them, "Unless I see the nail marks in his hands and put my finger where the nails were, and put my hand into his side, I will not believe it."

John 20:25

Dan took a deep breath. He had decided that no matter what ridicule was ahead, he was going to start making a bolder stand for the Lord. He'd asked his brother, an employee at a Bible publishing house, to get him copies of the *Book of John*. A whole case had arrived that morning, so his brother certainly had done his part. Now Dan needed to do his. He planned to give a copy to all of the guys in his dorm. He had his speech well practiced: "Hi! My name is Dan, and I live down in Room 101. This past spring, I found out that God loves us so much, he sent his son to earth. So I'd like you to read this book that tells about that. If you ever want to talk about it, like I said, I'm in Room 101."

He filled his backpack, took a deep breath, and opened his door. As he handed out the little book, some of the guys accepted it reluctantly. Others commented, "Right on. I read my Bible too."

But one resident, Randy, seemed especially interested. "Hey, thanks," he said. "I bought a Bible once, but it was too confusing to read. Maybe I can handle it in chunks like this."

Dan waited for several days, but hadn't heard from Randy even though they both usually returned from their last class about the same time. Dan glanced at the clock. It was 4:00 and the café didn't open until 5:00. That would give him an hour to see if Randy had any questions. "Help me not be stupid, Lord," he whispered as he opened his door and started down the hall.

He was surprised at Randy's welcome. "Hey, I'm glad you stopped back," he said. "This is an interesting little book. I'm from East LA, and my parents were part of a weird cult, so we never talked about this stuff. They always told me the only god that means anything is the god within us. I always thought that was weird because their marriage was a mess, all their friends were a mess, and I knew I was a mess."

Randy shrugged as he continued. "So I figured if we all have god in us, it's a god who doesn't have any power."

Dan was trying to think of what he was supposed to say, but Randy went on. "I guess, though, what's been the toughest was having two cousins taken out by a rival gang."

He thrust out his hands to show the tattooed letters above his knuckles. "The first cousin that got killed gave me these, saying they would identify me as belonging to the right family," he said. "But instead, those tattoos are what got him killed when he was on a bus where two rivals were. His tattoos didn't save him. Mine probably won't either if I ever go back to LA."

Randy shook his head as though ridding himself of a bad memory. "But I'm interested in what this book said about Jesus," he continued. "He didn't have tattoos, but he still died. Is it for real that he came back to life after he'd already been buried?"

Dan nodded, relieved he could answer that question, and opened the *Book of John* to the twentieth chapter.

"Yeah, that's true," he said. "Remember reading here in verse 10 about Jesus appearing to Mary in the garden when she was crying because she thought he had stayed dead? Well, that's told in other books of the Bible too. I'll make sure you get a whole Bible and I'll show you where the other books talk about it."

Randy took the book. "Wait. I read something in here; maybe he did have tattoos." He pointed to verse 25. "See? When his friend Thomas talks about wanting to see the nail-marks in his hands. I guess those were God's tattoos, huh?"

Dan swallowed. "Well, I never thought of it exactly like that," he said. Then he smiled and said, "But sure. Why not?"

The important thing was that Randy was on his way to the truth.

TO PONDER

- Do you have any experience with gang members? If so, what was the situation?
- Why do you think anyone would join a gang?
- Are you surprised Randy talked so openly about his background? Why or why not?

MAKE A PERSONAL CONNECTION ON DAY 9

Saul is jealous of David: 1 Samuel 18:5–17
Stephen is stoned: Acts 6:8–15; 7:52–60

ENCOUNTER STORY

> *His word is in my heart like a fire, a fire shut up in my bones. I*
> *am weary of holding it in; indeed, I cannot.*
>
> *Jeremiah 20:9*

This has pretty much been my life verse since I became a Christian twenty-three years ago. I had never read the Bible until then, but I quickly fell in love with the Old Testament and was absolutely enthralled to find all God has done in history.

When I found this verse, I was taken by the context of Jeremiah's confession that obeying God had been a real pain. Every time he did what God told him to do, things got worse. Jeremiah was mad at God and basically said, "I quit." But then he discovered God's Word wasn't just something he obeyed, it was something he had become. He couldn't quit because God had placed a fire inside of him. The heart of God lived inside of the heart of Jeremiah. Burning within him was the passion of God. God's burdens were his burdens. And so to his own amazement, he discovers, "but if I say, 'I will not mention him or speak any more in his name,' his word is in my heart like a burning fire, shut up in my bones. I am weary of holding it in; indeed, I cannot."

Jeremiah expresses my own experience. I never needed a seminar to coax me or motivate me to begin telling others about Jesus. From the moment I came to faith, it was like a burning fire that began to burn within me. I couldn't keep it in. This verse reminds me to keep the fire burning.

Erwin R. McManus, Lead Pastor
Mosaic Church
East Los Angeles, California

10 *Emotional Healing*

The thief comes only to steal and kill and destroy; I have come that they may have life, and have it to the full.

John 10:10

Lee paced the twelve feet of her private hospital room, running her hands through her disheveled hair as she waited for her appointment with the psychiatrist. Already, she didn't like this place, but since the voices had started telling her to hurt herself, her parents had insisted their family doctor get her immediate help.

The voices had started quietly enough—telling her she was no good. That she was fat. That she'd never have any friends. That the only people who were interested in her were ones who wanted to use her. Then the voices had gotten louder until the most soothing one had encouraged her to slash her skin. That command so frightened Lee that she told her mother about it.

Tears sprung into her mother's eyes as she whispered, "We're going to get you help, honey."

Lee continued pacing. Some help this was, being locked in a twelve-by-twelve-foot room. But they had assured her it was only until she could have her interview with the doctor, who could then analyze her specific needs and help her. She looked out the window through the mesh reinforcements and watched the morning staff go to their cars.

Am I ever going to get my life back? she wondered.

Just then, the door opened to admit the ward nurse.

"I'm here to walk you down to Dr. Patterson's office," she said. "It's not too far, but we have time to chat on the way if you want. It's up to you."

Lee shook her head. She was afraid to start talking. She was afraid she wouldn't be able to stop. The nurse slowed her steps to match Lee's.

"Are you scared about meeting the doctor?" she asked.

Lee started to shake her head no, then reconsidered and nodded.

"He's a good guy," the nurse said. "He just wants to talk to you and find out what things frighten you. It's right here. You'll be fine."

The nurse then opened the door to a large sun-filled office. The doctor stood up, put his hand out to her, and said, "Lee, I'm glad we're meeting. I want to help you, and I can best do that if you'll tell me about these voices you've been hearing."

Lee looked at him for a long moment trying not to hear the voice that said, "He's a con-artist; don't trust him."

She sat in the chair he offered, her back straight, her face tense.

"If you'd like, you may just sit there," the doctor said. "We don't have to talk today."

She shook her head. "No, I guess I wanna talk if it will make the voices stop." She ran her hands through her hair again.

"All right," he said. "Let's begin."

That would be the first of her daily sessions with the doctor. Along with taking medications, she met with him to talk about everything—the kids at school, what she was afraid of, and, finally, what the voices told her.

As the doctor began to talk about ways she could strengthen herself against the voices, Lee suddenly asked, "What do you do when you have bad thoughts?"

He paused for only a moment. "I quote Scripture in my mind," he said. "And I sing hymns in my mind. When I'm feeling anxious, I sing to myself: 'Jesus loves me, this I know, for the Bible tells me so. Little ones to him belong; they are weak, but he is strong."

Lee giggled. "But, you're a grownup."

The doctor smiled. "Yes, but even when we're grown up, we have times when we feel like a child. So I sing. And I quote in my mind encouraging Scripture. One of my favorites is Philippians 4:8: 'Whatever is true, whatever is noble, whatever is right, whatever is pure, whatever is lovely, whatever is admirable—if anything is excellent or praiseworthy—think about such things.' I quote that to myself and then concentrate on all the things in my life that are 'noble, right, pure, admirable, excellent, and praise-worthy.'"

"That's a really cool verse," she said.

"If you'd like, I can write it out for you, and you can think of all the good things in your life too whenever you're frightened."

"That'd be good," she said. Then she thought for a moment. "And maybe you could ask my mom if she's got a Bible I could read."

The doctor nodded. "I'll be happy to ask her," he said. "But if you don't want to wait, I have a Bible here you're welcome to have."

She nodded eagerly as the doctor opened his desk drawer. "This will give you an additional source of strength and encouragement in the days ahead. We're going to continue to do our part to help, but when you're frightened or feel alone, look for verses that talk about peace and strength and joy."

He opened to the back of the Bible. "This list in the back is called a 'concordance,' and you can look up different words—such as *peace*—and it will show you where you can find verses about that topic."

Lee nodded, hopeful for the first time in a long time.

TO PONDER

- What do you think about counseling and medication for Christians suffering from psychiatric problems?
- Do you wish this doctor had done anything differently?
- Do you know anyone who is struggling with emotional problems? If so, what help would you like to see offered?

MAKE A PERSONAL CONNECTION ON DAY 10

Healing power: Luke 8:40–56
Esther is called to help: Esther 4:1–17

ENCOUNTER STORY

You yourselves are our letter, written on our hearts, known and read by everybody.

2 Corinthians 3:2

Each week, 4.1 million volunteers teach the Bible in Sunday school, and I'm often one of them. I have a passion for teaching the Bible, and my own enthusiasm is fueled by the stories other volunteers tell about what keeps them coming back week after week.

One teacher told me about a four-year-old who made a mistake on her verse recitation. She piped, ". . .that whosoever believeth in him should not perish but have ever laughing life." Her teacher didn't correct her.

She told me, "I think Jesus loves having his little ones look forward with smiles and giggles to life with him."

Another teacher told me, "I was standing in the back of my church wondering if all the Sunday sweat was worth it." She smiled as she continued, "God let me hear his answer. One of my kindergartners ran up to his grandmother and announced, 'I learned a new verse.' He recited it for her and then much to his surprise she recited it back to him. 'Wow, Grandma, do you know any more?' he wanted to know. For the next few precious minutes they recited God's Word back and forth to each other, one verse after another. The only difference was that the grandmother recited from the King James Version and her grandson had memorized his from a modern language Bible."

Recently, I was teaching the story of Jairius's daughter to youngsters who were more familiar with the occult than the Bible. When I came to the part where Jesus raised the child from the dead, a nine-year-old blurted out, "Who taught Jesus such strong white magic?"

Teaching is not the only volunteer job in the church— just the most exciting and dangerous. We answer questions that can lead children to our resurrected Lord. We encourage early discipleship steps. What an opportunity! I celebrate with teacher Paul when he says to his Corinthian class: "You yourselves are our letter, written on our hearts, known and read by everybody. You show that you are a letter from Christ, the result of our ministry, written not with ink but with the Spirit of the living God, not on tablets of stone but on tablets of human hearts."

Marlene LeFever, Director of Church Relations
Cook Communications
Colorado Springs, Colorado

11 *Five-Cent Hot Dogs*

Then Jesus declared, "I am the bread of life. He who comes to me will never go hungry, and he who believes in me will never be thirsty."

John 6:35

Just after 10 A.M. on occasional Saturdays, John Paul unfolds an eight-foot table in front of his used tire store in West Warwick, Rhode Island, stacks Bibles and tracts on top, then brings out a long extension cord to attach to the electric hot plate filled with hot dogs. Finally, he positions a large sign that reads, RHODE ISLAND HOT DOGS—FIVE CENTS. He is ready for business.

He doesn't have to wait long. His first customer of the day is usually an elderly woman who lives in a tired looking apartment building across the street. She shows up at 10:30, plops down her nickel, then says, "You have the best hot dogs around."

But new customers gesture toward the sign with a gruff, "What's the catch?"

"No catch," John always answers.

"So why you doing this?" they ask.

"I'm just going about my father's business, and he wants me to provide both kinds of food—physical and spiritual," John says as he points to the hot dogs and Bibles to emphasize his point.

"So, who's your father?" is the invariable question.

By now, John has placed a plump frankfurter into a soft bun and hands it to the customer.

"My father is God," he says simply.

At this point, some customers hurry away with their inexpensive lunch. But most stay, asking more questions as they dab mustard into the bun.

"I had a great dad when I was growing up," John says. "And I learned how important it is to have a good relationship with my father. But he died when I was eleven. My mother wasn't around, so I grew up on the streets."

Often the listener will interject his own story then, and tears follow. Other times, John is encouraged to continue and he adds the reason behind the five-cent price of the hot dogs—the day he skipped school in 1958. He was fourteen and had been on his own for three years and was labeled a habitual runaway. That morning, he strolled by a greasy spoon restaurant that catered to blue-collar workers. The sign in the window read, SPECIAL TODAY. HOT DOGS. FIVE CENTS.

John was always hungry, but he didn't have five cents, so he kept walking. However, that hunger stayed with him throughout his teens and into adulthood and saw him doing well in any business he put his hand to. Still, no amount of material accumulation ever seemed to be enough, and it was as though he was trying to fill his long-ago empty stomach. In fact, it seemed the more he acquired, the emptier he felt. Then through a bad business deal, he lost several million dollars almost overnight. Gone were the fancy cars, the flashy clothes, and the high-rise apartment.

Thus, on the evening of September 8, 1994, he sat alone in his sparse trailer. Feeling totally at a standstill, he considered everything he had acquired—and lost—and wondered why he had even bothered. He felt very much like that kid who didn't have the nickel for a hot dog. Gradually, he realized the answer to his emptiness could only be God.

Suddenly he jumped up and shouted, "God, I'm getting out of this tonight, and I'm going to wind up with you or I'm going the other way. I'm done with it."

Then for the next hour, he continued to yell—and curse—at God, emphasizing his father's heart attack death that had devastated John's life. Finally, in agony, he threw himself on the floor, spread eagle, and cried.

He doesn't know how long he stayed with his face pressed into the carpet, but finally he said aloud, "Christ Jesus, you can have a crack at me. I've given everybody else, including myself, a chance, but look where it's gotten me.

So you fill me up, take away the emptiness. This is going to be my last shot to succeed as a human."

As he prayed, the most amazing thing happened: it felt as though—one by one—cement blocks were being lifted from his back.

The next morning, John couldn't wait to buy a Bible. As he began to read, he saw again and again that good deeds would not get him into heaven, and his accumulation of things would not fill his emptiness. His only hope was to accept the work Jesus had done on the cross, recognize him as his personal Savior, and confess that lordship with his whole being. When John realized Jesus is the only way into his heavenly Father's house, he pondered the idea that Christ came to serve and not be served. Suddenly, John's life took on new meaning—he had the same opportunity.

As he started a used tire business, he pondered ways he could use it to help hurting people. As he thought of ways to give hope and encouragement, he remembered the day he didn't have money for the hot dog. But knowing pride might keep people from accepting free food, he settled on the 1958 price.

Today, at his business, hot dogs not only fill an empty spot in stomachs, but they provide a way for him to talk about the Word of God that will fill emptiness in hearts. Furthermore, he has hung brightly colored signs from the ceiling that offer eye-catching encouragement such as "God's never busy. Give him a call." Or "Pray about everything. Worry about nothing." And stacks of Bibles are displayed wherever there's room. Many times customers will come in for a set of used tires and say, "Oh, yeah. You're the guy who gives away Bibles." John is known for more than just his good deals on merchandise.

"I didn't stay in school," John says. "But all the knowledge in the world doesn't mean a thing unless you apply it. Jesus *talked* to people. So we have to talk to people too about the relationship we have with our heavenly Father. Providing five-cent hot dogs and Bibles is one way I can tell people what God has done for me."

TO PONDER

- Have you ever achieved a goal that wasn't as fulfilling as you had planned? What happened?
- What advice do you have for others who are working hard to accumulate material goods?
- What opportunities do you have to share the Lord's reality through your daily life?

MAKE A PERSONAL CONNECTION ON DAY 11

Committing plans to the Lord: Proverbs 16:3–8
Foolish planning: Luke 12:15–21

ENCOUNTER STORY

> *One thing I ask of the Lord, this is what I seek: that I may dwell in the house of the Lord all the days of my life, to gaze upon the beauty of the Lord and to seek him in his temple.*
>
> *Psalm 27:4*

Psalm 27:4 has not always been my favorite verse of the Bible, but it has come to be so in the last several years. Perhaps this is because I'm past fifty, fast approaching sixty, and have lost several close friends and family members in the last two years. I find I am contemplating life more seriously the closer I get to the end of my own days, and I have examined the lives of those closest to me—many of whom were not believers. What was so important to many of these people—in fact, the things they chased their entire lives—did not matter a bit when they became sick and faced death. They were filled with fear and had no hope in an eternal life with a living Savior.

One relative, who had immense pride in her home and its furnishings, said bleakly to me in our last conversation together, "When you look at what I'm looking at now, none of those things matter. I don't even care what happens to my belongings; they don't matter."

What is so incredible about the Lord's Word and makes it so precious to a believer is that the Lord doesn't hide the future from us! To die is really to *live* . . . with a beautiful Savior in a beautiful place he has prepared for us! That is something to hope for and something the world does not value. But that reality is something the saints have staked their lives on for the past two thousand years.

Diane Passno, Executive Vice President
Focus on the Family
Colorado Springs, Colorado

ENCOUNTER STORY

> *"For I know the plans I have for you," declares the Lord, "plans to prosper you and not to harm you, plans to give you hope and a future."*
>
> *Jeremiah 29:11*

In our marriage ceremony, before the births of our children, at church and school, and at every turn of life, my wife, Elsie, and I had presented ourselves for God's service. Comfortably committed to God's will, we would apply that experience to others in church relations. The challenge came after forty years of pastoral life to move into unknown territory—the unique business world of parachurch organizations. Life after the age of sixty requires stewardship in personal responsibilities that will not be put off. But with each new challenge—whether physical or spiritual—we seized upon this particular text as confirmation that God was lovingly in charge.

So personal was this experience with his Word that I was surprised the verse is popular with many of my peers.

As I consider the changes that have occurred over the decades, I'm convinced that turning aside to spectacular events may rob Christians of the glory of the ordinary. The power of the gas pedal that takes us to church, to the grocery store, to school, and to friends' homes is lost beside the thrust of rockets aimed at outer space. But both are equally important—even awesome—in shaping lives and character.

God is granting Elsie and me these "best of all" years to remind anyone who will listen of the glorious ways of our God. Now, at age seventy-seven, after more than fifty years of serving him, it seems as though the goodness of God just gets better.

David Wambaugh, Retired Pastor
Charlotte, North Carolina

12 *More Than Medicine*

*Do not be wise in your own eyes; fear the Lord and shun evil.
This will bring health to your body and nourishment to your
bones.*

Proverbs 3:7–8

Jik stirred his tea after removing the cup from the microwave.
What a pathetic substitute, he thought as he remembered his
mother's gracious manner as she served her family at each
meal. *But that was another time and another place.*

He thought of her herb garden that had produced exotic
leaves herbalists purchased for their elixirs. In fact, she was
the one who had encouraged him to study medicine.

He dropped the tea bag into the garbage can, remembering her death just a few months before Mao Tse-tung
came to power. He often wondered what she would have
thought about the way he idolized their charismatic leader,
who held their entire nation in his grip. Oh, how he had
believed in what Mao had taught. Now he was bitterly

disappointed as he realized what Mao Tse-tung's true motives were. Once Chairman Mao—Jik cringed to think he had called him that again—seemed to have all the answers.

Now, after numerous years of a thriving oncology practice, Jik realized there were some areas of life no one had answers to—least of all medicine. He was especially interested in those supposedly hopeless cases where the patient who practiced prayer surprised the doctors by having, if not a complete recovery, at least extended life. He remembered one young father with advanced metastatic brain cancer whose church had put him on what they called a prayer chain and had prayed for him around the clock for three weeks. According to medical statistics, he should have died within the first two weeks but, amazingly, his cancer had gone into remission. There was no explanation in medical files for such a recovery.

Jik had discussed that case with Scott, another doctor.

"Well, I'm convinced Jesus is still the Great Physician," Scott had said. "And he's still interested in healing. He wants health for us, but our bad choices—and society's bad choices about everything from the air we breathe to the food we eat—will affect our health."

Jik had said, "You talk about this Jesus as though he's still alive."

Scott had nodded. "I'm convinced he is. My faith tells me he lived, died, rose again, continues to live, and wants the best for us. He's all powerful."

Jik smiled sadly. "All powerful," he repeated. "That's what the party leaders told us about Mao."

"I understand that," Scott said. "I've had a few of those types of disappointments myself over the years. But Mao was not truly interested in the people. He was interested in gaining power for himself."

Jik had nodded politely and changed the subject.

Now as he sipped his tea, he remembered that earlier conversation. *How can I explain I had trusted Mao to the extent that I never questioned anything he said?* He wondered. *Well, I learned a lesson. I won't be so foolish as to trust like that again.*

Just then Scott came into the break room and sat down across from Jik. "My wife and I are in a Bible study that meets every Thursday night," he said. "It's an open group, and you and your wife are welcome if you'd like to join us."

Jik looked up. "You are most kind to invite us. But we don't believe as you do," he said.

"Oh, that doesn't matter," Scott. "We've got a guy who claims he's an atheist and says he comes just to shoot holes in our theories. We put up with *him.* Actually, he makes us think, which I admit is a challenge for some of us."

Then Scott poked Jik on the arm, ignoring his cringe. "Hey, if nothing else, you'll get dessert afterward," he said. "And it will be a chance to meet more people. My wife and I have two-year-old twins, so she says it gives her a chance once a week to say more than "No, I said stop that."

Jik smiled, thinking of his own young son. "Perhaps my wife would like such a gathering," he said, ignoring his own curiosity. "But we don't own a Bible."

Scott shrugged. "No problem," he said. "We always have extras for visitors. But wait a minute. Let me get you one right now."

He walked to his locker and pulled his copy off the top shelf. "This week, we're discussing the three parables—uh, stories—in Luke 15. Here, I've marked the chapter. Luke was a physician too, so I especially like his observations about the activities of Jesus."

Jik nodded. "Thank you," he muttered politely as he accepted the Bible Scott held toward him. *But I will not believe about this Jesus. I have been disappointed enough,* he thought.

"Remember, tell your wife no pressure. We just talk about Jesus and how he helps us deal with the stuff in our lives."

Jik nodded politely again, determined not to get into a debate. He didn't realize he had already started a two-year search that would end with his daring to trust again.

TO PONDER

- Have you ever put your faith in someone who proved untrustworthy? If so, how did that affect future relationships?
- What suggestions do you have for well-meaning people witnessing to those who have been betrayed?
- Would an unbeliever be welcome in your Bible study group?

MAKE A PERSONAL CONNECTION ON DAY 12

A health need: Matthew 9:12
A son restored to life: 2 Kings 4:35

ENCOUNTER STORY

On a Sabbath Jesus was teaching in one of the synagogues, and a woman was there who had been crippled by a spirit for eighteen years. She was bent over and could not straighten up at all. When Jesus saw her, he called her forward and said to her, "Woman, you are set free from your infirmity." Then he put his hands on her, and immediately she straightened up and praised God.

Luke 13:10–13

As a medical doctor, I'm fascinated by the healing miracles of Jesus. The New Testament contains forty-two such accounts, but I'm especially drawn to the miracle of Luke 13:11. Often Jesus was *asked* to heal a person, but this is the only miracle where that does not happen. In this account, he sees a woman in the temple, totally bent over. We're told she had a spirit of infirmity for eighteen years, so I think of her in that culture. Since she would be like a hunchback who couldn't look people in the face, she undoubtedly experienced constant rejection. But on this Sabbath she is in the temple worshipping. In addition to being brave enough to venture outside her home, she is faithful to worship and faithful to God despite her circumstances. No one asked for her healing on her behalf, but Jesus knew her heart and healed her.

We read this account quickly and take for granted the total and immediate healing. But as a doctor, I think of what actually happened to her physically. Today with modern medicine, we can straighten people. However, it would take a *team* of neurosurgeons to straighten her spine; we'd have to have a *team* of cardiovascular surgeons to reposition her heart, along with a *team* of pulmonary surgeons to reposition her lungs. And that's just a start. There would be numerous follow-up surgeries to complete the healing, but Jesus did all that in an instant.

At the end of Matthew, we read, "Jesus did many more miracles." Thus, all that is recorded in these forty-two healing miracles is just a small glimpse of his healing power.

Linda Williams, M.D.
Family Physician
Denver, Colorado

13 *An Afternoon Walk*

*And I will pour out on the house of David and the inhabitants of
Jerusalem a spirit of grace and supplication.*

Zechariah 12:10

Hannah smiled as she lifted eight-month-old Aaron from his
crib. He grinned back at her, his two new bottom teeth shin-
ing. After she changed him, she settled into the rocking
chair. Cooing, he flailed his arms and legs in anticipation of
being fed. As she nursed him, listening to his little gulping
sounds, she thought about the conversation she and her
husband, Benjamin, had had at dinner last night.

At temple, the new rabbi had read from Isaiah 53:

*Who has believed our message and to whom has
the arm of the Lord been revealed? He grew up
before him like a tender shoot, and like a root out of
dry ground. He had no beauty or majesty to attract
us to him, nothing in his appearance that we should
desire him. He was despised and rejected by men,
a man of sorrows, and familiar with suffering. Like*

one from whom men hide their faces, he was despised, and we esteemed him not.

As she served the chicken and noodles, she had asked Benjamin who it was the rabbi had been talking about. At the temple, she sat in the back with Aaron and did not always hear the readings. Benjamin sat in the front where he could concentrate.

"He was talking about the Messiah who will come," Benjamin answered as he broke off a chunk of the *challah* bread.

"Did he say when the Messiah will come?" Hannah asked. "I've long wondered about that."

"Our people have always looked for the Messiah," Benjamin said. "Personally, I think Israel itself is the Messiah. Once the land totally belongs to us, we will realize that the Messiah has, indeed, arrived."

Hannah nodded. "Yes," she agreed. "But isn't the Messiah supposed to be one man?"

Benjamin took a sip of wine. "Don't use energy thinking about such things. Your job is to take care of Aaron and run our house. My job is to work and ponder such truths."

Now as she rocked Aaron before their afternoon walk, she tried to push down the feeling of irritation that Benjamin had told her not to think about something she had wondered about since she was a child. Aaron loosened his hold on her and smiled, signaling he was full. She turned him over and patted his back, still thinking about Benjamin's comments. Then she bundled Aaron into his blanket, put him in the stroller, and opened the door.

Just as they turned the corner, she saw two men talking on the sidewalk. She knew they weren't from the neighborhood, so she greeted them quietly as she passed with downcast eyes.

"Hello," they answered in unison. Then the taller of the two men held a book out to her. "Would you like a copy of the entire Bible?"

She glanced at him, then tightened her grip on the stroller handle. "Sir, I respect all religions and ask that you respect mine."

Immediately, he replied, "I have been rude. I should have introduced myself first. My name is Moshe. I too am Jewish, and I can do nothing but respect our people. But rabbinic Judaism has diverted from the revelation God gave our people in the Scriptures. I must respect his Word above the traditions of men."

Then he asked, "Would you be willing to look at what God says about who the Messiah is?"

Caught off guard, she stammered, "Yes," remembering her questions to Benjamin the night before.

"The Messiah has already come," Moshe said as he handed her a small Bible. "Look in the back," he continued. "It's a list of what our prophets said about the Messiah. The rest of the book contains Jewish text written by Jewish people about a Jewish issue. This little Jewish book has changed the world."

Moshe continued to hold the book out to her while Hannah stared at it. Finally, she looked directly at him.

"But is this something I should be reading?" she asked. "My husband says that is his job."

Moshe couldn't believe a woman of the twenty-first century was asking that question. "Don't let others hide the truth from you," he said gently. "Not even your husband. Look into the truth for yourself."

Hannah thought for a long moment, then accepted the little book and tucked it under the folds of Aaron's blanket. She hoped the book would explain the passage the rabbi had read last night.

TO PONDER

- Do you have friends outside of your own ethnic circle? If so, what have you learned from them?
- What do you feel they have gained from you?
- If you don't have friends from other backgrounds, would you like to? Why or why not?

MAKE A PERSONAL CONNECTION ON DAY 13

Promise to Abraham: Genesis 17:1–27
Descendants of Abraham: John 8:31–41

ENCOUNTER STORY

> *Here I am! I stand at the door and knock. If anyone hears my voice and opens the door, I will come in and eat with him, and he with me.*
>
> *Revelation 3:20*

This verse has been a favorite of countless people through the ages, and it certainly is for me. It was the verse that brought me to Christ more than fifty years ago, and I have seen people respond to Christ in all five continents as the impact of this verse has hit them as well. It is particularly effective for people who, like the Laodiceans, have everything—except Christ; or those who, like the Laodiceans, are supremely confident of their own achievements.

Michael Green, Canon
Advisor in Evangelism to the Archbishops of Canterbury
and York
Church of England
Oxford, England

14 Two Coal Miners

In your love you kept me from the pit of destruction; you have put all my sins behind your back.

Isaiah 38:17

The journey from the coal mines to the pulpit for Kentucky pastor Jerry Adkins began June 6, 1982.

"When I went to work that morning, I was a strong and confident thirty-two-year-old," Jerry says. "I didn't think much about the prayer session my wife, Jean, and her sister had had about me the night before. Jean was always praying for me. It was almost as though that was her job—just as mine was to get up at 4 A.M., be at the mine by 5:00, work all day under the mountain, come home, shower, eat dinner, drink while I watched TV, go to bed, and start the routine again the next morning."

But what he didn't find out until later was that Jean had cried out for God to save her husband—"whatever it takes."

So that morning when Jerry, the supply man, loaded his mining locomotive in preparation to drive to the face—the wall of coal being mined that day—he was just minutes away from God's answering his wife's prayer.

Alone, he stacked cinder blocks into the cars. Then to provide traction between the metal wheels and rails, he sprinkled sand on the rails, just as he did every morning. As Jerry climbed into the driver's seat, the machine caught on the sand, jerked, and threw him under its deadly wheels.

As the metal chewed into his skin, he cried out, "Lord, help me!" Suddenly he was tossed aside, his leg almost severed. Jerry would spend the next month in hospitals. The fifth day, he developed a pulmonary blood clot.

"I had to lie still with nothing to do but watch TV and think about my life," Jerry says. "And I kept thinking how I had cried out to the Lord to help me when I hadn't given him much thought before the accident.

"Sunday morning, I clicked the TV until I found a worship service," Jerry says. "As I listened, everything the minister said made sense. When he prayed for those who need a Savior, I said aloud, 'That's me, Lord. You saved my life, now save my soul.' And from that day on, everything changed."

When Jerry was released from the hospital, he still had fifty-two days of intense therapy waiting as he learned to walk again. It would be seven months before he went back to the same job, but he wasn't the same man.

"I couldn't talk about the Lord enough or read the Bible enough," he says. "Before long, I was taking classes so I could become a pastor."

When an offer to pastor a new church came, Jerry left the mines and set up his own sign-making business so he could accept. One of the first men he led to the Lord was Morris Thacker, a miner who had just buried his father.

His condolence call to the Thacker home lasted more than the twenty minutes he had planned. "As I started to leave, I handed Morris a pocket-sized New Testament," Jerry says. "Three hours later, we were still talking."

Morris threw out challenge after challenge, including questions about eternal security. Jerry turned to Scripture to answer each one.

Finally, Morris said, "I believe all that. I believe Jesus is the Son of God, that he was virgin born, died on the cross, went in the grave, and rose three days later. There has to be more to it than that."

Jerry replied, "Romans 10:9 says, 'If you confess with your mouth, "Jesus is Lord," and believe in your heart that God raised him from the dead, you will be saved.' I'm going to kneel right here and ask God to make the truth you've said with your mouth come alive in your heart."

He knelt by the sofa, and Morris and his wife, Rita, knelt too. Jerry prayed, but Morris kept thinking about how painful his inflamed knee was. At one point, Rita squeezed Morris's arm to let him know she was making a decision, but he was concentrating on his knee. At Jerry's *amen,* they rose to their feet.

"I didn't get a thing out of that, Preacher," Morris said.

"Well, you've got to pray yourself," Jerry replied.

"I pray every morning before I leave for the mine," Morris said as he escorted Jerry to the door.

The next day, as Morris climbed into his jeep, his knee was especially painful. He put his hand on it and said aloud, "God, I'm not asking for a miracle. I just want to be able to work and provide for my family."

At the mine, he limped to the mantrip—the vehicle transporting miners to their stations. As they disembarked, Morris slipped in mud and flipped backward.

That'll be the end of my knee for sure, he thought as he landed.

But as he pulled himself up, he realized he wasn't hurt. Amazed, he walked a little way; still no pain. Then as a further test, he jogged down to the power box several yards away. Still no pain. He smiled at his good fortune. Suddenly a voice deep within his spirit gently said, "You prayed for this."

His mouth flew open as he remembered how he had asked to be able to continue to work. Right there, in the mine tunnel, he dropped to his knees.

"Forgive me, Lord," was his earnest cry. And for the next several minutes, he confessed every sin that came to mind.

"Then I started thanking God for my family and for not giving up on me. I thanked him for everything from cereal to applesauce," Morris says. "I believe the Lord works with stubborn people in different ways. And I had been one of the most stubborn men around. All my head knowledge hadn't meant a thing until I got hold of it in my heart."

The next day, Morris started carrying the Bible Pastor Jerry had given him.

"It was so little I could put it in my dinner bucket," he says. "At noon, the other miners would kid me when they'd see me reading. But pretty soon they were asking where I'd gotten 'that little bitty Bible' and wanted one too."

To date, Morris personally has given more than five hundred Bibles. "I gave miners all the Bibles our church could spare as quickly as I could, then I started ordering them by the case. I even gave Bibles out at Halloween and to a guy who had stopped in my yard to ask directions."

Those who know mining is the second most dangerous job—right behind fire fighting—always ask what helps when he's working the shuttle car under the mountain.

"I don't know what helped me before I found Jesus," Morris replies. "Now, he works right beside me."

Morris is quick to turn conversation back to the Lord. "Before I got saved, I couldn't stand to read anything religious," he says. "Now I can't get enough of God's Word. In fact, I don't know what my wife and I talked about before we came to the Lord. We're all the time talking about what we've read that day."

Morris ponders for a moment. "I've found people are hungry to know God's Word," he says. "I believe we will be accountable for not telling people about Jesus. After all, if the disciples hadn't told folks about the Lord back then, where would we all be today?"

And to think all these changes began with one wife's plea for her husband's salvation.

TO PONDER

- Has God ever dramatically stepped into your life? If so, what was the situation?
- What helps you in today's day-to-day responsibilities?
- How do you share your personal faith with others?

MAKE A PERSONAL CONNECTION ON DAY 14

The importance of the Word: 2 Chronicles 34:14–27
The greatest offering: Mark 12:41–44

ENCOUNTER STORY

> *Though I am free and belong to no man, I make myself a slave to everyone, to win as many as possible. To the Jews I become like a Jew, to win the Jews. To those under the law I become like one under the law (though I myself am not under the law), so as to win those under the law. To those not having the law I become like one not having the law (though I am not free from God's law but am under Christ's law), so as to win those not having the law..To the weak I became weak, to win the weak. I have become all things to all men so that by all possible means I might save some. I do all this for the sake of the gospel, that I may share in its blessings.*
>
> *1 Corinthians 9:19–23*

Paul's words clearly speak to the need, particularly acute at the present time, to be open and embracing toward persons of other faiths, on the one hand, and fully faithful to the Gospel on the other. Churches seem to do fairly well on the first part—being all things to all people—but not so well on the second part—sharing the Good News. For some reason, Christians, whose lives have been restored to new life in Christ, are reluctant to share their faith. Yet there can be no greater act of love than such sharing. It is out of a deep conversion that Christians are empowered by the Holy Spirit to be loving toward others in a new and profound way. They become less emotional and defensive in dealing with persons of other faiths because they are secure in their own faith. A Gallup survey taken a few years ago showed that the vast majority of Americans say it is only by the grace of God they are truly able to forgive someone who has hurt them deeply.

George Gallup Jr, Chairman
The George H. Gallup International Institute
Princeton, New Jersey

15 The Best Race

Therefore, since we are surrounded by such a great cloud of witnesses, let us throw off everything that hinders and the sin that so easily entangles, and let us run with perseverance the race marked out for us.

Hebrews 12:1

Joanne propped open her door in welcome. As dorm senior resident, it was her job to welcome the freshmen who would be arriving within the hour. She counted the thirty-two information cards that had been sent ahead of their arrival. She was particularly interested in their list of hobbies and interests. She paused at Nancy's card when she saw that the freshman was attending on a track scholarship. Joanne smiled, remembering her own track days in high school.

But I certainly didn't win a scholarship, she mused. *Still, it will be fun to have that in common, so we'll have something to talk about.*

She made a mental note to seek Nancy out, but she didn't have to wait long. Nancy was one of those in-your-face personalities—full of questions and challenges and ideas of how everything could be done better.

No wonder she's on scholarship, Joanne often thought. *She's a born competitor.*

About three weeks into the semester, Nancy stopped by Joanne's room unexpectedly and saw the Bible open on the study desk.

"How come you're reading that?" she asked.

"The Scriptures give me encouragement for daily challenges," Joanne answered. "Besides, I like reading stories about how Jesus answered people who challenged him."

Nancy seemed especially interested in that. "Why would anybody challenge him?" she asked.

"Well, there were those who didn't believe he was the Son of God."

"Wait. You mean he actually went around saying he was the Son of God?" Nancy asked incredulously. "No wonder they challenged him."

Joanne took a deep breath. "He *was* the Son of God," she said.

Nancy sniffed. "I don't believe that. One of my teachers in high school said Jewish girls were always claiming to be pregnant with the Son of God when actually they had visited a Roman soldier's tent," she said.

"No, Jesus' birth had been prophesied in the Old Testament," Joanne answered evenly. "Isaiah said he would be born of a virgin, and the New Testament records that he was."

"This I've got to see," Nancy challenged. "But I'm gonna be late for class."

Joanne wasn't going to let her get away so easily. "How about if you stop by after dinner," she said. "And I'll show you the verses that talk about his birth." Then she added, "Make sure you bring your Bible."

Nancy chuckled. "Oh, that's a laugh; I don't have one."

Joanne tried to hide her surprise. "Oh. Well, you can use one of mine."

"Sure. See you later," Nancy said and hurried on to class.

As the door closed, Joanne said aloud, "What on earth have I done?" as she grabbed her Bible and a yellow legal pad and began listing verses featuring the virgin birth.

She turned first to Isaiah 7:14: "Therefore the Lord himself will give you a sign: The virgin will be with child and will give birth to a son, and will call him Immanuel."

Then she listed Matthew 1, verses 18, 20, and 23. Before long she had read the entire book of Matthew and then turned to the book of Luke, jotting down verse after verse she could show to Nancy. In the middle of her list making, there was a knock at the door.

At the answer of "Come in," Nancy peeped in. "I didn't see you in the cafeteria," she said. "Is this when I'm supposed to come?"

Startled, Joanne looked at the clock and realized she had been reading the Word right through dinner.

"This is a great time," she answered. "Here's my extra Bible. We'll start in Matthew."

Joanne waited for Nancy to open the Bible, then realized Nancy did not know the location.

This is going to be tougher than I thought, Joanne thought. Aloud, she said, "The Bible is made up of the Old Testament and the New Testament. Matthew is the first book in the New Testament."

She paused. Nancy continued to look at her. "The Old Testament tells about God creating the world and then records events that happened before Jesus was born," Joanne continued. "The New Testament starts out with four books called Matthew, Mark, Luke, and John."

She gently took the Bible off Nancy's lap and opened it to Matthew before handing it back to her.

"The first four books are about Jesus and what he did while he was here on earth," Joanne said. "The books that follow talk about him, but they are mainly principles of how we can live the way God wants us to."

Joanne swallowed hard; she wasn't sure she was saying this right at all. "What would you think if we just started by reading Matthew aloud," Joanne asked. "We can start at verse 18 since the first seventeen verses list the fourteen generations from Abraham to David. We can talk about those later."

Nancy remained quiet, so Joanne continued. "Let's start with the birth of Jesus," and she began to read verse 18. "This is how the birth of Jesus came about. His mother, Mary, was pledged to be married to Joseph, but she was found to be with child through the Holy Spirit."

This sure is a weird start, Joanne thought. *But it's a start. And this is going to be Nancy's best race ever.*

TO PONDER

- Have you encountered those who insist Jesus merely was born out of wedlock? If so, what were the details of the discussion?
- Why do you think it was important to Joanne that she have something in common with the incoming freshman?
- Is there anything you would have liked her to have done differently during this first Bible study?

MAKE A PERSONAL CONNECTION ON DAY 15

Joseph's forgiveness: Genesis 50:15–20
Jesus in the Garden: Mark 14:32–41

ENCOUNTER STORY

Thanks be to God for his indescribable gift!

2 Corinthians 9:15

This is the verse that ties together America's two most revered holidays—Thanksgiving and Christmas—and our Christian faith. On the one day, we thank God for blessing our nation, and on the other we celebrate our Savior's birth.

In 1935, at age eleven, I welcomed that indescribable gift into my own life when I accepted Jesus Christ as Savior. It was the message of God's gift of love to mankind in John 3:16 that touched my heart to believe. In the sixty-six years since that miracle in my life, I've been prompted to underline verses listing the blessings this Gift gives to me. Here are a few:

1. Forgiveness: *1 John 1:9 and Colossians 1:14*
2. Salvation: *John 3:17, Romans 10:13, and Ephesians 2:8*
3. Eternal Life: *John 3:15 and Romans 6:23*
4. Heaven: *John 14:2–3 and Acts 1:11*
5. Peace: *John 14:27, Romans 5:1, and Philippians 4:7*
6. Reward: *Matthew 5:12, Luke 6:23, Hebrews 11:6, and Revelation 22:12*
7. Comfort: *2 Corinthians 1:3 and 2 Thessalonians 2:16–17*
8. Wisdom: *Psalm 111:10 and James 1:5*

9. Inheritance: *1 Peter 1:4, Romans 8:17, Hebrews 9:15, and Titus 3:7*
10. A New Body: *1 Corinthians 15:44 and Philippians 3:21*
11. Blessings: *Malachi 3:10, Ephesians 1:3, and Matthew 5:8*
12. And many, many more, including *1 Corinthians 2:9 and Ephesians 3:20*

Philip W. Hirschy, Retired Science and Math Teacher
Evans City, Pennsylvania

ENCOUNTER STORY

> *My dear brothers, take note of this: Everyone should be quick to listen, slow to speak and slow to become angry.*
>
> *James 1:19*

This passage suddenly appeared in my Bible in 1990. As an educator, I subtly had been taught that I had the answers and should be in control. Administratively, I was always ready to defend teachers and policies. After all, we had the answers and certainly, in the matter of schooling, we were the ones to be in control.

Then through this Scripture, the Lord taught me the most powerful and effective professional lesson I have ever learned. Suddenly, with my new understanding, I found that as I listened, without defense or excuse, to the offended or angry person, I was able to resolve the conflict in a gentle and winning way. After all, once the offended person has been heard, he or she seems to move easily toward problem resolution. Most interestingly, I also discovered that being quick to listen makes it easy to be slow to speak.

Ken Smitherman, President
Association of Christian Schools International
Colorado Springs, Colorado

16 The Bible Bike

John Britz, known as "Traveling John," pulled his motorcycle near the food tent at the Lake George, New York, rally. Only 50,000 bikers were expected to attend—far less than the number who crowded the streets of Sturgis, South Dakota, and Laconia, New Hampshire, each year—but John takes as many opportunities as he can to share the Good News.

And the "Bible Bike," as his 1994 Honda Gold Wing is called, is an immediate attention grabber since scenes from Genesis to Revelation are airbrushed in color over the entire shiny black surface—including Adam and Eve in the Garden, Noah's Ark, the parting of the Red Sea, the Nativity scene, the woman at the well, Jesus praying, his crucifixion, heaven, and hell.

John set a box marked "Free Bibles" on the back of his Honda, then unfolded the literature rack he had made and arranged yellow and black tracts in the slots.

"I don't push Bibles on people because I didn't like it when people pushed me before I became a Christian," John says. "I just have them available along with tracts in our Pittsburgh sports team colors of yellow and black. I also have a pamphlet explaining all the bike's airbrushed scenes."

Next to the tracts are books of yellow and black matches, which display a picture of a motorcycle on the front and "Follow the Son"—the name of John's ministry— on the back. Inside is the poem his wife, Karen, wrote:

This match can light the darkest night,
Yet soon its glow is gone.
But day or night, there's one true light
That burns on and on and on.
Jesus—the Light of the world, John 8:12

"I go through almost 5,000 books of matches a year," John says. "Of course, some people criticize me for giving them away, saying I'm encouraging smoking. But what I'm interested in is providing something the bikers will use— and be reminded of Jesus in the process."

John first started giving away Bibles in 1990. "I didn't have the system worked out yet, though," he says. "That first year I gave away thirty *large* Bibles. The next year I'd caught on to the need for smaller ones, and I gave away a hundred. Now I easily give in the summer months alone 15,000 pieces of literature, including 4,000 Bibles."

John has put more than 370,000 miles on his motorcycle and has been riding for almost four decades—eleven years longer than he's been a Christian.

"A fellow at work who really knew the Word had been quietly witnessing to me and got me thinking about going to church. So when a new one was built near us in the fall of 1977, Karen and I decided to check it out. Before Christmas, we both accepted the Lord."

"Up until then, my motorcycle was my god," he says. "I never thought you could ride and be a Christian too. So when I accepted the Lord, I decided that was the end of my riding days. I guess I had seen too many Christians living under the law who didn't do anything fun on Sundays, but then their actions the rest of the week would make up for any goodness they had tried to display earlier."

That thinking was changed by a beautiful spring day.

"One Sunday morning, the weather was so great I suggested to Karen that we ride the bike to church," John says. "I was ready for rude comments from folks, but nobody said a thing. After church, we rode to the mountains and talked about the sermon. I gave up my god for the real God, and he has let me ride my bike more and more."

After a 1986 trip he and Karen had taken to Alaska, John had realized his dream of traveling throughout all fifty states on his motorcycle. The only thing left to do then was attend a rally.

"I figured I wouldn't fit in with the guys anymore; still, I wanted to be around others who enjoyed motorcycles as much as I do. But I got lost outside of Baltimore and couldn't find the rally. I stopped at a crossroad to get my bearings and sat there with my Follow the Son sticker on the back of my bike and 'Jesus' stitched on my saddle bags."

Then another bike pulled up, and the rider, Ivan Stubbs, asked if John was going to the rally. At his affirmative reply, Ivan said, "Praise the Lord; you can help me with the church service."

The rally was held in an old fruit orchard that contained a barn. Ivan walked into the musty building, straightened a couple of tables, put away the beer cans, and started singing.

"Just the two of us were there," John says. "But when Ivan sang 'Unto Thee, O Lord, do I lift up my soul,' four people wandered in. They stayed to listen to his short sermon, and then all four accepted the Lord. I was hooked on ministry right then."

During the next year and a half, John took his vacation time from his Export, Pennsylvania, factory job to attend rallies with Ivan as part of the Motorcycles for Jesus ministry. Sometimes rallies would be held on conflicting dates, so Ivan would take one state and John another.

"Pretty soon I was confident enough to go out on my own," John says. "Now I just hang around my bike and talk to anybody who stops by. When they comment on the various scenes, I explain the reason why I chose each one."

From there, conversation often turns to news of the latest accident since the largest rallies seem to produce at least one fatality.

"If you're a biker, you know you might not make it home that night," John acknowledges. "So when we talk about the accidents, I ask right out, 'If you don't make it home tonight, where are you going to wind up—heaven or hell?' Some walk away at that point, but others say, 'Well, heaven.' Of course, I ask 'Why?' and the usual answer is, 'Because I believe in God.'

"Well, even Satan believes in God," John replies. "From there, I've got an open door to tell my testimony and explain how Jesus Christ is the only way to heaven."

One biker with whom he had that conversation was Mark, a big guy from New England, who rode a Harley Davidson Shovel Head. He and his two buddies had wandered past John's bike and commented on the scenes, but didn't stay to talk. About thirty minutes later, Mark was back—alone.

"You're not going to convince me about this Jesus stuff," was his immediate challenge. Then he called himself a heathen and rattled off his mixture of beliefs that included reincarnation.

"Okay, let's just talk," John replied.

And for the next hour—before Mark's buddies came looking for him—they talked about everything from Mark's family to John's testimony. As they shook hands goodbye, Mark pulled a Bible out of the box with the promise to read it. John nodded, but he knew Mark's best ride ever was about to begin.

TO PONDER

- What has been your experience with motorcycles?
- What scenes would you choose to airbrush on the Bible Bike? Why?
- How do you use your interests to witness for the Lord?

MAKE A PERSONAL CONNECTION ON DAY 16

Choose righteousness: 1 John 5:18–21
Parting of the Red Sea: Exodus 14:5–31

ENCOUNTER STORY

> *For when David had served God's purpose in his own genera-*
> *tion, he fell asleep; he was buried with his fathers.*
>
> Acts 13:36

I have just completed my twentieth year at Dallas Seminary. From this perspective, it seems I've been around here a long time. My plans (not necessarily God's) are not to retire until age seventy or even later (another thirteen years plus). After all, how could the seminary operate without me? At the same time, it's a sobering thought to know that some day I'll be gone, and I'll not be here to make a difference as I challenge our students to serve Christ in church revitalization and planting. It's when my thoughts are working along this line that God brings to mind Acts 13:36: "For when David had served God's purpose in his own generation, he fell asleep; . . ." That's my goal in life, to serve God's purpose, and then leave the results to him. He's using me now in this generation, and he will bring others along in the next generation to have a high impact for him.

Aubrey Malphurs, Church Planter and Author
Dallas Seminary
Dallas, Texas

ENCOUNTER STORY

> *But you are a chosen people, a royal priesthood, a holy nation, a people belonging to God, that you may declare the praises of him who called you out of darkness into his wonderful light. Once you were not a people, but now you are the people of God; once you had not received mercy, but now you have received mercy. Dear friends, I urge you, as aliens and strangers in the world, to abstain from sinful desires, which war against your soul. Live such good lives among the pagans that, though they accuse you of doing wrong, they may see your good deeds and glorify God on the day he visits us.*
>
> *1 Peter 2:9–12*

The words in 1 Peter 2:9–12 speak right to my heart about my place in the family of God. It reminds me who I am and Whose I am—I am his and he is mine!

I have been saved, redeemed, and cleansed by his precious blood. What a personal delight to know from these verses that Jesus Christ is the precious "cornerstone" of my heart and life. That understanding leads to my daily desire to be a living stone for him and allow him to build the house of my heart and soul. My passion and desire are to be the man God wants and needs me to be.

God reminds me in these verses that as believers we are (1) a chosen people, (2) a royal priesthood, (3) citizens of a holy nation, and (4) his own special people. What a bless-ing these promises from his Word are in my daily life. My esteem and self-worth truly are found in him and not in any-thing in this world. I do not want to conform to this world, but rather I want to be transformed by my God. I am the child of a King! Hallelujah!

Major Steve Owen, Pastor
The Salvation Army
Colorado Springs, Colorado

17 The Right Decision

This day I call heaven and earth as witnesses against you that I have set before you life and death, blessings and curses. Now choose life, so that you and your children may live.

Deuteronomy 30:19

Colleen picked at her dusty rose nail polish as she waited for Susan to come back into the room with the results of the pregnancy test. *My senior year was supposed to be my best year yet,* she thought. *How could I have been so dumb?*

She was editor of the newspaper, captain of the pom-pom squad, and steady date of the school's star linebacker, who was slated for an All-State position. Life should have been perfect. Now here she was in the office of the local crisis pregnancy center.

At first, she had to deny the obvious symptoms, telling herself she'd been exercising too much lately for her body to function normally and that the late-night pizza while working on paper deadlines caused her to have an upset stomach in the mornings. Then she saw the ad that began simply, "Afraid you might be pregnant? Come in for a test—free and confidential."

The following afternoon, after telling her mother she needed the car to do research at the library, she showed up at the address listed on the ad. The receptionist had greeted her warmly and then escorted her down the narrow hallway to meet Susan, who smiled as she extended her hand.

Now, Colleen glanced toward the door, wondering how much longer Susan would be. How could she tell her parents? They'd been so proud of her. And what about the college scholarship? And what about Mike? He wasn't going to be happy at all. Colleen shredded the tissue in her hands.

The door opened, but Colleen didn't bother to turn. Susan sat next to her and took her hand.

"You are pregnant, dear," she said. "But you already knew that, didn't you?"

Colleen nodded as the tears ran down her cheeks.

"Will your boyfriend be supportive?" Susan asked.

Colleen shook her head. "No, this will mess up his plans."

"What about your family?" Susan asked.

Colleen couldn't get the words out fast enough at how disappointed they would be. They'd had such wonderful plans for her. Now this.

"Do you have a church family who will be supportive during this time?"

Colleen shook her head. "We don't go to church much," she said. "Just holidays and stuff. We're always so busy."

Then she raised her eyes to Susan. "What am I going to do? I've messed up so many lives." She paused, then asked, "Do you guys, like, do abortions?"

Susan spoke slowly. "No, we don't provide abortions," she said. "We try to help you see all the various choices you have, then we will support you in whatever decision you make. But along with the other information, we provide you with what abortion means physically and emotionally. You wouldn't have any other kind of surgery without getting the facts about what all is involved and how long it will take to recover. So we want you to have information about abortion too. We understand the pressure from others for you to have an abortion, but this decision must be one you have chosen."

"I've really messed up my life, huh?" Colleen asked.

"God brings his good out of whatever situation we give him," Susan replied. "And he gives us opportunities to start over. Do you have a Bible at home?"

Colleen shrugged. "I don't know. I guess so."

"Would you like one to help you through the next few days as you think about what you're going to do?"

At Colleen's nod, Susan opened the desk drawer. "Here's a New Testament. It's called *Hope for the Future* because the material in the front will encourage you that your life is not ruined."

Colleen accepted the small book as Susan continued. "In fact, I've marked a passage in Psalm 139 to remind you that God hasn't forgotten you or your baby."

Susan waited a long moment, then asked, "Are you comfortable telling your parents tonight or would you like me to go with you?"

The teen shook her head. "No, I'll tell 'em. We're all gonna cry, though."

"Crying is a good thing at a time like this," Susan said. "But I want you to know we can help you with doctor's appointments. And all our services are free. Even the ultrasound, should you decide you want to see the size of your baby. From what you've told me, you're probably about seven weeks along, so your baby will show up nicely."

Colleen sighed. "My *baby*. Yeah, I've got a lot to think about. But first I better tell my folks."

Susan escorted Colleen to the door, again emphasizing her availability. Then after she waved goodbye to the girl, Susan went back to her chair, put her head on her desk and whispered, "Help her choose your way, Father."

While Susan prayed, Colleen sat in the car reading the first page. *Four Little Words: "I think I'm pregnant." I had never been in this situation before, and I just couldn't believe it.*

Colleen sighed. Maybe she wasn't alone after all.

TO PONDER
- Do you know anyone who has faced a crisis pregnancy?
- What choices were available?
- What choices were made?
- What advice do you have for those who are in a similar situation?

MAKE A PERSONAL CONNECTION ON DAY 17

The unborn child: Psalm 139:13–16
Love worth waiting for: 1 Corinthians 13

ENCOUNTER STORY

> *Only be careful, and watch yourselves closely so that you do not forget the things your eyes have seen or let them slip from your heart as long as you live. Teach them to your children and to their children after them.*
>
> Deuteronomy 4:9

Early in my single parenting days, a summer trip to South Dakota showed me a way to lock God's miracles and promises into my children's hearts. As we approached the spectacular landmark of Mount Rushmore, we saw a sign that said, "Historical Marker Ahead."

I pulled the van to a stop. On a bronze plaque, we read how Gutzon and Lincoln Borglum carved the faces of four presidents into the granite of the Black Hills mountain over a fourteen-year period. That site became more than a tourist stop for us after we read the marker—it became a timeless memorial.

That evening in our hotel as we continued to talk about the bronze plaque, I opened our Bible to the Exodus account, where we read that Moses was one of the first who left behind a commemorative memorial. He had tried to get Pharaoh to let the Israelites leave slavery and go into the land God had promised them. When Pharaoh refused, God sent plague after plague upon the Egyptians, climaxing with the promise that the firstborn of all animals and humans would die. That night, Moses instructed the Israelites to put blood on the tops of their doorposts so the angel of death would "pass over" them, further adding, "Obey these instructions as a lasting ordinance for you and your descendants. When you enter the land that the Lord will give you as he promised, observe this ceremony. And when your children ask you, 'What does this ceremony mean to you?' then tell them, 'It is the Passover sacrifice to the Lord, who passed over the houses of the Israelites in Egypt. . . .'" (Exodus 12:24–27).

After reading the Exodus account, we searched for other passages reporting the creation of markers created by individuals to commemorate events they did not want successive generations to forget. Then we talked about the ways in which God had been with us during our tough times. What had started as a mere family vacation became the foundation for our own faith-building adventure.

Dr. Lynda Hunter, Former Editor
Single-Parent Family Magazine
May 1995 "Well Spring" column

18 Two Paychecks Away

The King will reply, "I tell you the truth, whatever you did for one of the least of these brothers of mine, you did for me."

Matthew 25:40

Bob stretched, then pulled his jacket from under his pillow. The shelter's rules were firm: in by 7:30 P.M. and out by 7:45 A.M. It was time to get going for the day. He folded the bright pink blanket with the tattered binding that had been donated to the shelter, then groped under the cot for his boots. He had been fortunate last night to get a cot next to the wall, so he had pushed his boots into the farthest corner for safe keeping. He smiled as he double tied the laces. One of the workers had dumped them into the shelter's shoe bin right at the moment he was sorting through the various boots. He had grabbed them, delighted they were only a little big. Two pairs of heavy socks took care of that.

Bob bent under the cot again to pull out a plastic two-gallon bucket that contained a sponge and a roll of paper towels. When he had found the bucket by the dumpster behind the tire shop, he'd carried it all day, thinking of ways to use it to make a little money. Now, after a breakfast of oatmeal and coffee at the shelter kitchen, he would hit the streets and offer to wash the windshields of the morning shoppers. He'd tried hanging out at the library like many of the other homeless, but the rule was that you had to be reading. No naps were allowed, and the reading rooms were too warm for the layers of clothing he wore. So he saved the library visits for snowy days.

He hadn't meant to wind up on the streets like this. He thought about the apartment he and Margaret had rented when they first moved to town. Housing was tight, so when the landlord raised the rent for the second time in eight months, Bob's check just couldn't cover it. They'd talked about Margaret getting a job, but her salary would have been eaten up in child care. He'd always heard that the common worker is two paychecks away from the street. Well, now he had proven that to be true. Margaret tried to stick it out with him, but when his job was eliminated after the September 11 attacks, she took their little girl and left. They didn't have much in the way of furniture, so when the landlord handed him the eviction notice, Bob gathered his few articles of clothing and walked out the door.

He'd lived on the streets for a couple of weeks before— when his step-dad kicked him out on his eighteenth birthday. Now here he was again, having to learn the ropes in a new town. The main shelter served breakfast, but only to those who had stayed the night. Otherwise, you had to go to the city recreation center. In the winter, they tried to serve oatmeal, but sometimes all they could offer was cold cereal. But at least the coffee was hot. Lunch and dinner were at the church soup kitchen down the street. Oh, the church didn't call it a "soup kitchen," and the folks were nice enough, but he'd never known spaghetti could be served so many different ways.

He'd tried hanging out at the day labor office, but the group there was growing while employers needed fewer part-timers. He'd tried to get a real job, but employers like to see a permanent address on the applications. So here he was, trying to wash a few windshields for a buck or two. Enough to call Margaret's parents to see if she and the baby were there. But he dreaded to talk to her dad since he reminded him so much of his step-father. Well, maybe he'd earn enough to get a bus ticket to a new place—a warmer one.

Panhandling in this town could land a person in jail. And even with the free meals that would be provided, jail time was not something he wanted on his record. By now he had walked to his favorite station in front of the used book store. The folks who went in there usually stayed for a while, so they were more prone to agree to a washed windshield.

"Wash your windshield for a buck or two while you shop, ma'am?" he would say. And he'd always smile. But no matter how they answered, they'd seldom look him in the face.

"Hey, I used to be just like you," he'd want to yell. "I used to buy books too." But that would only frighten them.

So he'd stand by the little alley between the book store and the music shop, with his hands in his pockets. Occasionally some softhearted woman would hand him a dollar whether or not she wanted her windshield washed.

All day, he waited, hands in pockets. *Don't think about tomorrow, just get through today* was his motto. He watched a matron in a Buick Park Avenue pull up in front of the book store. But her car was spotless. No need to even ask. But, nevertheless, he smiled and said, "Good day, ma'am."

She turned, startled at his voice, but replied, "Oh, yes, hello to you too." Then she opened the door of the book store.

Boy, she was a million miles away, he thought. *I wonder what she was thinking about. It sure wasn't me.*

He stayed at his post until he heard the Westminster chimes of the nearby church strike 4:45. Well, time to meander on over for supper. *And I haven't earned even a buck today. Oh, well.*

Just as he dumped the water into the alley, he heard a timid voice behind him. "Young man?"

He turned to see the owner of the Buick standing at the entrance to the alley. "Yes?"

"I wanted you to have this—maybe to read to pass the time. And I thought maybe you might need a little cash to tide you over for a day or two."

He looked at what she held out to him—a pocket-sized New Testament, with a $20 bill sticking out of its pages. Then he realized she was looking him directly in the face.

Now it was his turn to be startled. "Thank you, ma'am. That's kind of you."

As she got into her car, he waved goodbye, then opened the Bible to pull the bill out. *Maybe it's time I called Margaret,* he thought.

He stared at the Bible. *Gosh, how long has it been since I've read this?* Then he sighed. *Maybe it's time I started.* And with that he picked up his bucket, squared his shoulders, and walked to the waiting spaghetti dinner.

TO PONDER

- What is your experience with the homeless?
- Do you agree the common worker is two paychecks away from the street?
- Do you agree with the Buick owner's action? Why or why not?

MAKE A PERSONAL CONNECTION ON DAY 18

An unlikely source: Joshua 2:21
The woman at the well: John 4:3–18

ENCOUNTER STORY

> *But seek his kingdom, and these things will be given to you as well.*
>
> *Luke 12:31*

In 1969, my wife, Annette, and I felt led to an Abrahamic phase of life, so we bought an old school bus and converted it into mobile living quarters. We felt our ministry Scripture was Luke 12:31 and that we were to learn how God answered prayer and could provide for us if we brought our needs to him privately. Our first stop was a mission at Kayenta, Arizona.

When our time there was drawing to a close, we realized we needed additional storage room for Annette's Vacation Bible School supplies. We decided to ask the Lord for a travel trailer that could be pulled behind the bus. We made this known only to him. We asked for an empty 20–24 foot-long aluminum travel trailer. We figured 20 feet was the minimum amount of space we needed, and 24 feet was the longest we should tow behind the 31-foot long bus.

Approximately six weeks after we began praying for this, a man approached me one Sunday morning and said, "I have a trailer for sale in Window Rock, and as I was praying last night, the Lord told me to give it you. Do you want it?"

I asked, "How long is it?"

He said, "Twenty-four feet. Aluminum."

Goose bumps jumped out all over my body, and I almost pinched myself to see if this was a dream. We towed the trailer behind the bus for several months until the Lord led us to give it to Rick and Marlene, a young couple who had come out of the Hippie settlement to travel with us and be discipled. They were living in it at a ministry where we were working, but when we felt God was telling us to move on, they felt led to stay until after the birth of their baby. So Annette and I privately asked the Lord for a sign that we were to give the trailer to them permanently.

Then, a family came to visit from Southern California and had hauled supplies for the ministry. When they got ready to leave, I told the husband I would hook his box trailer back to his car.

He said, "That isn't my trailer anymore; God told me to give it to you."

All of Annette's materials fit perfectly in the new trailer, which came with a sturdy tarp cover so everything stayed dry. Again God had provided his solution, and we left our first trailer with Rick and Marlene.

After a few months, they felt they were to rejoin us. They had traded the travel trailer for a 24-foot-long converted school bus and called to say they were coming. As it turned out, I was going to be in their area, so I would travel back with them. We took off from Oregon with enough groceries for the trip and $35 to spare. We had 1,100 miles to travel, but gas was only 19–21 cents per gallon back then. Besides, it would be interesting to see how God provided.

We had driven only one full day when the engine began knocking, signaling that a rod bearing had gone out. We were in the mountains in northern California parked uphill on the shoulder in the rain. The baby began crying, and everything looked pretty bleak. We were praying when a knock came at the rear door of the bus.

Standing in the rain was a young man asking if we needed help. We explained the engine situation, and he offered to tow us. Before towing, though, he opened his trunk and pulled out a can of used oil and added it to his engine. As he pulled the bus, smoke literally poured from underneath his car to the point he had to stick his head out the window for air. But he got us to the next town and introduced us to the local mechanic. We insisted he take $20 for towing us. We now had $15 remaining.

The mechanic checked the engine and gave us the news it would take $135 to repair it. When I had begun this trip, I had left Annette and our children in Flagstaff, where she was volunteering at a local Bible book store. I called her there to let her know our situation. I had left her with $15, so there was little hope she could help. I just wanted her to know where we were and what to pray for. But, as it turned out, she had her own adventure happening.

Earlier that week, a businessman had come into the book store asking for material about living by faith. Annette referred him to George Mueller's books, but when he said he wanted more current stories, she shared some of God's provision for us. A few days later, this businessman sent her a check for $135, which arrived on the same day I called about our $135 repair! The bus was repaired, and we made it safely to Flagstaff with an empty gas tank and empty pockets.

During our first months in Albuquerque, before Hosanna began, I had been witnessing on the streets and teaching in home meetings. After a few weeks we were not having our needs met. I went to the Lord, stating that if our needs were not being met, it had to be one of three reasons: I was fired, I was not seeking his kingdom, or he had gone broke. I reasoned he was not broke and I had not been told I was fired, so I asked him if I was not seeking his kingdom and doing what he wanted me to do.

His answer surprised me, "I am speaking to my people here to provide for you, but they are too immature to respond."

I rejected this answer—thinking it was simply my desire to give myself approval. But when I finished my prayer time and returned to the bus, I was met by our oldest son.

He said, "Tom drove up and gave me a $100 bill."

Tom, a sensitive servant, had told the Lord he would give it to me tonight at the prayer meeting, but the Lord told him to do it immediately. So Tom jumped in his car and drove right over. Not only did God let me know I was to keep working for him in Albuquerque even though things might get a little tight, but he let me know he will continue to take care of our needs as long as we keep presenting them to him.

Jerry Jackson, Founder
Hosanna
Albuquerque, New Mexico

19 The Rude Student

But while he was still a long way off, his father saw him and was filled with compassion for him; he ran to his son, threw his arms around him and kissed him.

Luke 15:20

Kyle wasn't one who would hold another's attention for long. He was tall and sullen, and his habit of staring over the head of anyone who might try to engage him in chitchat certainly discouraged friendship.

Usually, he strode into his university lectures just ahead of the professors, but one morning, he appeared early for his first class and sprawled in his usual chair near the door. A gregarious classmate seated nearby nodded in greeting, then gestured toward the philosophy text Kyle always carried on top of his stack of folders.

"Which philosopher do you like best?" he asked.

Kyle merely shrugged. Clearly, he did not want to start a conversation.

But the next week, just before the semester ended, the campus Bible club invited a professor from the philosophy department to speak to their group. So, Kyle's classmate, a regular attendee, invited him along.

The day had been especially dull, and Kyle was bored and looking for an argument, so he went. If they had been giving awards that night for rudeness, Kyle would have won. He often interrupted the speaker by throwing out the name of an opposing philosopher. Later, during the coffee hour, he gave a loud hurumph in answer to those students who commented on how informative they found the lecture. Then he ridiculed the entire concept of such meetings.

"How can one claim intelligence while attending meaningless lectures and believing principles from an archaic text?" he scoffed.

Most of the students cast disapproving glances his way as they moved away, but one young woman dared to challenge him.

"Actually, you're the one who's showing ignorance," she said. "You ridicule a book you haven't read."

She turned to the stack of student Bibles on a nearby table. "Here, take this," she insisted. "After you've actually read some of it, you can express an opinion."

Kyle was not used to being challenged, and she had caught him off guard. Thus, without argument, he accepted the volume she thrust into his hands and grumpily thumbed through the pages. The study notes caught his attention immediately, but when he realized several students were watching him with interest, he tossed the Bible onto a nearby chair and strode out the door.

The following Thursday evening at the campus coffee shop, Kyle ran into his classmate again, who promptly asked him to the weekend Bible Conference. To both of their surprise, Kyle accepted.

The first night, he sat slumped in his seat, his long legs thrust in front of him, his arms folded across his chest. The second night, he sat straighter but he often looked around as though studying the other attendees.

The third night, he actually opened the Bible his classmate offered and followed as the speaker read the account of the prodigal son in Luke 15. Suddenly, Kyle began to read ahead, excitedly flipping through the entire book of Luke. Every few minutes throughout the sermon, he would elbow his fellow student, gesture toward a miracle or parable and say, "Have you seen this?"

Kyle had suddenly discovered the Bible wasn't boring, and he found life beyond what he had known. The one who had once been hostile to the book he didn't understand now couldn't wait to introduce it to others.

TO PONDER

- How do you explain Kyle's sudden passion for Scripture?
- Have you ever experienced a similar insight?
- How do you react to those who challenge your intelligence because you read the Bible?
- How would you like to respond?

MAKE A PERSONAL CONNECTION ON DAY 19

The prodigal son: Luke 15:11–24
Joseph meets the brothers who sold him into slavery: Genesis 42:6–17

ENCOUNTER STORY

I have made you known to them, and will continue to make you known in order that the love you have for me may be in them and that I myself may be in them.

John 17:26

I'm often asked how I came to this ministry of presenting the Bible dramatically. That's a long story, but the capsule version is that drama, theater, and storytelling is the medium that God has used in my life to fulfill my desire to make Christ known.

I fully accepted the reality of Jesus after I read parts of the book of Galatians and all of John's Gospel in one sitting.

The story of Jesus in John was so gripping that I thought Jesus was going to come right out of the pages of the Bible and take me with him. When I got to the account of his death on the cross, I was in tears. I saw the sacrificial love and I responded to Jesus emotionally and immediately. Only later, when I sat under teachers and professors, was I able to explain what happened to me. But at that time, I knew instantly that Jesus' death on the cross and his resurrection was supremely important to me. I knew I would never again be the same.

I had a similar reaction the first time I read Genesis. The hugeness and audacity of the first book of the Bible is just overwhelming. Genesis is filled with massive personalities that made an extraordinary impression on me. But what really struck me is how God interacted with them personally. Genesis showed me that God is personal and involved in our lives, directing the course of events to a particular purpose for his glory and our ultimate good.

I think what motivated me to memorize books of the Bible, such as Mark's Gospel, Genesis, and the Acts of the Apostles, and to present them dramatically, was a deep desire to recapture and share those powerful initial experiences I had with the God of the Bible. I want to share my personal experience that, though I am more sinful and weaker than I ever imagined, in Christ I am more loved and accepted than I ever dared to hope.

The Bible is its own evangelist. I came to faith because of how deeply the words of the Bible hit me. Charles Spurgeon got it right when he was asked how he defended the Bible. "Very easy," he responded. "The same way I defend a lion. I simply let it out of its cage." When I tell a Bible story, I have a quiet confidence that God is going to do a mighty work—by the very act of unleashing his Word. Therefore, my objective is to engage my hearers and draw them into the Word of God.

Recently I had a discussion with my lighting designer. In the course of our interchange I asked him, "If you died tonight, would you go to heaven?"

He answered, "I used to think so until I started working with you."

By hearing the message, he came to understand his need for a Savior. That need led directly to an intense discussion about Jesus and his grace. He believed and trusted in what Jesus did for him on the cross.

From time to time I get letters that say, "I came to faith because of listening to or seeing your presentation of the Bible." Others say, "That verse you gave today on the radio really convicted me. I need to deal with that."

When I get these responses, I know it is not me, but the Lion of God's Word doing its powerful work.

Max McLean, President
Fellowship for the Performing Arts
Morristown, New Jersey

20 No More Fear

I sought the Lord, and he answered me; he delivered me from all my fears.

Psalm 34:4

Duc clawed the blanket away from his face, then awakened with a start. Dazed, he looked around the hotel room, then realized where he was. He was a computer programmer attending a week-long conference in Dallas. No longer was he a frightened eight-year-old back home in Korea. He drew a long breath, remembering those long-ago nights when everyone was asleep, but he would lie awake, watching the shadows. Nighttime had always been difficult, but after his grandfather's death, he wondered what it was like to disappear from the earth. In those moments, his heart would begin to pound so intensely, he could hear the *lub-dub* sounding in his ears. Then his chest would tighten, making it hard for him to breathe.

Think of beautiful things, he would tell himself. *Think of Grandfather's gardens.*

Still, images of fire-breathing dragons and two-headed snakes would come each time he closed his eyes. He would hold his breath, wondering if snakes were slithering across the floor toward his sleeping mat.

Where will I go if I'm not here? he asked himself. *Will monsters eat my heart?*

He had tried once to explain his terrors to his parents, but they had dismissed his fears.

"Be strong and control your thoughts so that you might control your fate," his father said.

Still the fears had persisted throughout his childhood. And now they had followed him to the Dallas conference.

He got out of bed and felt his way to the comfortable chair near the window, careful not to awaken his roommate. *Perhaps I'm just nervous because of the program schedule,* he thought.

The nightmares increased. Finally, the night before the proficiency exam, Duc sat at the desk in his room, sipping tea and trying to stay awake. His roommate was at a Maverick's game with friends. They had invited Duc, but he had begged off, saying he needed to go over his notes. He yawned and looked longingly toward his bed, but nighttimes again had turned into the terrors they had been for him as an eight-year-old. He opened the drawer to get stationery to write his parents, but shut it instead. He couldn't write his parents. His parents had always said he had to be in control of his fate. Well, he wasn't in control of his fate.

In fact, he couldn't even control what was happening to him this week.

He looked at the book on his roommate's nightstand. He had asked Duc on the first day of the program if he knew the Lord.

At Duc's reply of "I worship the Lord Buddha in my ancestor's temple," the roommate had gulped and changed the subject. Now Duc wondered who his roommate's Lord was. Even back home, he had heard of the secret Great Power. Was that his roommate's Lord?

He sat for a long moment, thinking about his nightmares. Then timidly, he slid off the chair to kneel on the floor, touching his forehead to the carpet.

"Secret Great Power, are you so great that you can help me?" he asked. "If you are, I want to know you."

Duc held his breath, hoping for an audible answer. But none came. As he raised his head, he glanced toward the book his roommate read each morning.

Perhaps the secret power would be found in those pages, he thought.

Duc thumbed through the book's thin pages until his eyes fell on John 14:27:

> *Peace I leave with you; my peace I give you. I do not give to you as the world gives. Do not let your hearts be troubled and do not be afraid.*

Duc was startled by the words. Then, wondering who was speaking, he started at the beginning of chapter 14:

"Do not let your hearts be troubled. Trust in God; trust also in me. In my Father's house are many rooms; if it were not so, I would have told you. I am going there to prepare a place for you. And if I go and prepare a place for you, I will come back and take you to be with me that you also may be where I am. You know the way to the place where I am going." Thomas said to him, "Lord, we don't know where you are going, so how can we know the way?" Jesus answered, "I am the way and the truth and the life. No one comes to the Father except through me."

Each word seemed to speak directly to Duc, and he tried to sort out the new thoughts: "Trust in God" and "I am the way and the truth and the life." *The secret Great Power has a name!* he thought, and he felt his heart swell with a strange joy and peace.

Duc continued reading, occasionally glancing at the door. He couldn't wait until his roommate returned; he had so many questions.

TO PONDER

- What do you imagine Duc said when the roommate returned?
- Based on his earlier reaction to Duc's confession about worshipping the "Lord Buddha," how do you think the roommate reacted to his questions?

- Have you ever been startled by questions about your faith? If so, what helped you prepare for the next such event?

MAKE A PERSONAL CONNECTION ON DAY 20

The Lord's deliverance: Psalm 34:7
Jesus walks on the water: Matthew 14:23–33

ENCOUNTER STORY

*Fear not, for I have redeemed you; I have called you by name;
you are mine. When you pass through the waters, I will be with
you; and when you pass through the rivers, they will not sweep
over you. When you walk through the fire, you will not be
burned; the flames will not set you ablaze. For I am the Lord,
your God, the Holy One of Israel, your Savior.*

Isaiah 43:1–3

The date was March 13, 1977, and I was with a short-term
mission team from Greater Europe Mission, doing church
planting in Rome. At the end of the three years, I was coor-
dinator of discipleship ministries for the team, which consisted of eighteen missionaries involved in street work in a
new housing zone. We would meet the Italians through
open-air meetings that consisted of music, pantomime or
drama, and testimonies. The Italians are used to street meetings, though theirs were usually political, so a group always
gathered quickly. Our goal was to meet the people and
eventually be invited to their homes for Bible study where
we could train the men who would become the church eld-
ers when we left the country.

As we were coming to the end of this project, the director with whom I had been working was being sent to New
Jersey to train short-term missionaries, and he asked me to

join him and head up personnel and training. He needed my decision by the following Monday.

So, on March 13, a Sunday as I recall, I drove my tiny and very slow two cylinder Fiat 500 to a city park. The team called my vehicle "The Duck" since, in addition to its "yellow ducky" color, its previous owner had pasted a decal of a water fowl on the back bumper. When I stood next to it, the car came up only to my waist, so driving it was like running around in a washing machine. But the car and I made it to the park, where I pulled under the shade of two large cedar trees to read my Bible. On Sundays back then, most of the town took an afternoon stroll with their families. A woman sitting alone in a car was unusual since women didn't do things alone. So people stared at this tall woman sitting in a little car with her Bible propped up on the steering wheel. But I quickly forgot about their curiosity.

"Lord, what shall I do?" I prayed. "I need something to cling to—something I can come back to that will make sense out of whatever happens."

As I prayed, I began thumbing through the Old Testament. Suddenly Isaiah 43:1–3 caught my attention, especially the part about the rivers and the fire, since it had been emotionally fiery in Italy.

"Well, Lord, this is good stuff," I whispered. "But how does this relate to my question about moving?"

I chuckled when I realized I actually wanted a Scripture that would tell me to go to New Jersey. But as I continued to ponder the verse, I realized this would be my foundation.

God would be with me, and whatever was ahead would not be bigger than what he and I could face together. The important thing was not my job, but to know him. That would be the filter through which everything had to go.

Mim Pain, President
WorkPlace Influence
Colorado Springs, Colorado

21 A Troubled Marriage

If we confess our sins, he is faithful and just and will forgive us our sins and purify us from all unrighteousness.

1 John 1:9

Rodney, the executive director of the help center, smiled as he stood to extend his hand to Rachel and Glen. They both carried filled shopping bags, so he knew they already had received food and, perhaps, clothing from one of the counselors. But they had asked to see him about more serious matters.

As he gestured to the two chairs positioned in front of his desk, Rodney said, "I haven't seen you folks in a while. What brings you here today?"

He studied the couple as he waited for them to speak. Rachel was petite with long black hair that hung down her back. She was dressed simply for the chilly spring day and wore a light sweater and blue jeans. Her husband, Glen, sat slumped in the chair, his set jaw framed by shoulder length brown hair and his face prematurely lined like that of a heavy drinker. His black vest was stained, and his faded blue jeans were stuffed into unpolished biker boots. But it was the despair on their faces that held Rodney's attention. Truly, if ever a couple presented a picture of hopelessness, Glen and Rachel did.

From their previous introductory meeting, Rodney knew they had been married for twenty-seven years and, like other couples starting out, thought by the time they had reached middle age they would be financially secure. Instead, Glen's seasonal construction work and—Rodney suspected—his drinking always kept them off balance.

Finally, Glen cleared his throat and said, "We're in a tough spot with our marriage."

Rachel's head was still down, but she nodded. Gradually the details came out. Rachel had developed an adulterous relationship with one of the workmen at their apartment complex. When the affair ended, she had been so guilt-ridden she had asked for a divorce.

Glen, of course, was hurt, but didn't want a divorce even as he added, "I don't know why you had to go with that scum."

Rachel sighed. "You were always out with your drinking buddies. I got lonely. Besides, he was always saying he liked my hair. You never even look at me anymore."

"Sure, I do."

"Well, nice to tell me now. Anyway, I told you I'll give you a divorce."

"And I told you I don't want one."

Rachel lifted her head. "But how can you live with me now?" she asked. "How can you forgive me? I can't even forgive myself."

Rodney leaned forward to interrupt. "Rachel, have you asked God for forgiveness?" he asked.

"What's the use?" she managed. "There's no forgiveness for women like me."

The director opened the Bible on his desk. "Let me read a story to you from Luke chapter seven about a woman who was a sinner too."

As he read the account of the woman weeping behind Jesus and then pouring perfume over his feet and wiping them with her hair, Rachel shifted uncomfortably in her chair.

Rodney continued, "Then Jesus said to her, 'Your sins are forgiven.' Rachel, he's offering that same forgiveness to you, if you'll ask for it and then accept it as she did."

Rachel puffed out her cheeks but said nothing.

Rodney sat quietly for a moment, then turned to Glen. "While Rachel thinks about forgiveness, let's talk about your drinking."

Glen shrugged. "Drinking makes it easier to face my problems."

Rodney had heard that before. "Look, Glen," he replied in his no-nonsense way. "You can blame an abusive childhood, manipulative relatives, harsh bosses—you name it—and it still comes down to this: You made the choice to face your problems with the bottle and now you're hooked. You don't drink because you have problems; you have problems because you drink."

Rodney spread his hands wide. "I grew up in the home of an alcoholic, and I've learned there are few things more complicated than the life of an alcoholic and the way he affects those who love him."

"Hey, I can control my liquor," Glen retorted.

Rodney didn't even pause. "The key word for anyone who is addicted is *control.* And as long as you are fighting for control of your drinking, you're losing. It's only when you admit you *can't* control it that you will begin to win the battle."

He continued. "Addiction is something we can't fight by ourselves. Addiction brings loss of free will, and we wind up feeling the way Paul described in Romans 7:19–20."

He turned pages in the Bible. "Listen. 'For what I do is not the good I want to do; no, the evil I do not want to do— this I keep on doing. Now if I do what I do not want to do, it is no longer I who do it, but it is sin living in me that does it.' Sounds like a good definition of addiction to me."

He closed the Bible. "And since we can't fight an addiction alone, I always recommend AA or the program at my church that will help you learn new ways to cope with life's challenges. You've been handling life's challenges with booze. When you decide to choose a new life, you'll have to learn a new set of rules. And that can be frightening."

Glen frowned. "Do I look like I'm afraid of anything?"

Rodney didn't flinch. "Yes, you do, Glen. You're afraid of losing control—control of yourself and control of Rachel."

He held out the Bible. "We're going to pray for mutual repentance and forgiveness in a moment, but I want you both to start reading this," he said. "Read the Book of Mark together since it presents miracles of Jesus in a straight-forward manner. Then, Rachel, I want you to re-read Luke 7 and think about that woman weeping at the feet of Jesus. And, Glen, I want you to read the Book of Hosea since it is, about the prophet's determination to remain faithful to his unfaithful wife."

He paused, then added, "You both can have that new start. But it's up to you."

As Glen took the offered Bible, he thrust his other hand toward Rachel, who clutched it. They were willing to make that new start.

TO PONDER

- If you are married, what has been your toughest challenge?
- How have you faced it?
- If you are single, what action from a spouse do you think would disappoint you the most?
- What individual issues are you working on?

MAKE A PERSONAL CONNECTION ON DAY 21

Mary wiping the feet of Jesus: Luke 7:36–50
Words of love: Song of Songs: 2:16–17

ENCOUNTER STORY

> *Do not fret because of evil men or be envious of those who do wrong; for like the grass they will soon wither, like green plants they will soon die away. Trust in the Lord and do good; dwell in the land and enjoy safe pasture. Delight yourself in the Lord and he will give you the desires of your heart. Commit your way to the Lord; trust in him and he will do this: He will make your righteousness shine like the dawn, the justice of your cause like the noonday sun. Be still before the Lord and wait patiently before him; do not fret when men succeed in their ways, when they carry out their wicked schemes.*
>
> *Psalm 37:1–7*

My dad died when I was seventeen; my mother died ten years later. When I married Billye Joyce Vance, her dad and mother became very close to me. Then Mr. Vance's health began to deteriorate, and soon he died too.

At the time, Billye Joyce and I were serving as Christian education specialists for the International Center for Learning (ICL). During our training session that summer, Rev. Earl Lee led devotions and walked us through Psalm 37:1–7. That Scripture was so meaningful to us, and it has became our philosophy of life for the past thirty years. Committing to God—palms down—whatever problem or burden that is giving us pain or grief is the first step of living a victorious life. Next is trusting God, leaning hard on him, and believing he will help us through the experience as he has promised. Then, delighting in God, looking up and thanking him in advance for the first glimpse that shows us who he is and what he does. Finally, resting, being still, and knowing he is God allows us to be confident of his solid control of our situation, which allows us to rest in him.

No matter what the circumstance has been in our lives, these principles for victorious living have helped us work through whatever comes our way. And we know this cycle will greatly benefit anyone who follows this special Scripture passage. We know from experience that one can get out of the cycle at times, but God allows each of us to re-enter at any point and become refocused.

With God and his Word, we can overcome adversity and accomplish anything!

Dr. W. Edward Fine, Senior Minister
Downtown Christian Church
Johnson City, Tennessee

The 21 Day Bible Encounter

Day 1	John 19:17–37 Psalm 22:18	The crucifixion of Jesus Scripture fulfilled
Day 2	1 Samuel 17:32–50 Nehemiah 4:14–20	David meets Goliath Rebuilding the wall
Day 3	Judges 6:12–7:9 John 21:1–14	A weak man made strong Jesus fills the nets
Day 4	Genesis 21:8–21 Matthew 1:18–24	Hagar and her son, Ishmael The birth of Jesus
Day 5	Genesis 1:1–31 2 Timothy 1:1–12	The creation One of Paul's prison letters
Day 6	Exodus 3:1–14 Matthew 13:1–23	The burning bush Parable of the sower
Day 7	Mark 10:17–29 Psalm 73:24	Rich young man God's counsel
Day 8	Matthew 11:1–11 Exodus 2:1–15	Jesus and John the Baptist The early life of Moses
Day 9	1 Samuel 18:5–17 Acts 6:8–15; 7:52–60	Saul is jealous of David Stephen is stoned
Day 10	Luke 8:40–56 Esther 4:1–17	Healing power Esther is called to help
Day 11	Proverbs 16:3–8 Luke 12:15–21	Committing plans to the Lord Foolish planning

Day 12	Matthew 9:12	A health need
	2 Kings 4:35	A son restored to life
Day 13	Genesis 17:1–27	Promise to Abraham
	John 8:31–41	Descendants of Abraham
Day 14	2 Chronicles 34:14–27	The importance of the Word
	Mark 12:41–44	The greatest offering
Day 15	Genesis 50:15–20	Joseph's forgiveness
	Mark 14:32–41	Jesus in the Garden
Day 16	1 John 5:18–21	Choose righteousness
	Exodus 14:5–31	Parting of the Red Sea
Day 17	Psalm 139:13–16	The unborn child
	1 Corinthians 13	Love worth waiting for
Day 18	Joshua 2:21	An unlikely source
	John 4:3–18	The woman at the well
Day 19	Luke 15:11–24	The prodigal son
	Genesis 42:6–17	Joseph sold into slavery
Day 20	Psalm 34:7	The Lord's deliverance
	Matthew 14:23–33	Jesus walks on the water
Day 21	Luke 7:36–50	Mary wiping the feet of Jesus
	Song of Songs 2:16–17	Words of love

How to Get
Connected When —

YOU FEEL ABANDONED

Psalm 119:105   Your word is a lamp to my feet and a light for my path.

Isaiah 41:9   I took you from the ends of the earth, from its farthest corners I called you. I said, "You are my servant"; I have chosen you and have not rejected you.

Isaiah 54:5   For your Maker is your husband—the Lord Almighty is his name—the Holy One of Israel is your Redeemer; he is called the God of all the earth.

Philippians 4:19   And my God will meet all your needs according to his glorious riches in Christ Jesus.

Hebrews 13:5   Keep your lives free from the love of money and be content with what you have, because God has said, "Never will I leave you; never will I forsake you."

1 Peter 5:7   Cast all your anxiety on him because he cares for you.

YOU FEEL CONFUSED

Psalm 37:5–9   Commit your way to the Lord; trust in him and he will do this: He will make your righteousness shine like the dawn, the justice of your cause like the noonday sun. Be still before the Lord and wait patiently for him; do not fret when men succeed in their ways, when they carry out their wicked schemes. Refrain from anger and turn from wrath; do not fret—it leads only to evil. For evil men will be cut off, but those who hope in the Lord will inherit the land.

Psalm 121:1–2   I lift up my eyes to the hills—where does my help come from? My help comes from the Lord, the Maker of heaven and earth.

Proverbs 3:5–6   Trust in the Lord with all your heart and lean not on your own understanding; in all your ways acknowledge him, and he will make your paths straight.

Proverbs 16:3   Commit to the Lord whatever you do, and your plans will succeed.

Jeremiah 33:3   Call to me and I will answer you and
tell you great and unsearchable things
you do not know.

Philippians 4:6–7 Do not be anxious about anything, but in
everything, by prayer and petition, with
thanksgiving, present your requests to
God. And the peace of God, which transcends all understanding, will guard your
hearts and your minds in Christ Jesus.

Hebrews 13:8   Jesus Christ is the same yesterday and
today and forever.

YOU FEEL LONELY

Psalm 5:3   In the morning, O Lord, you hear my
voice; in the morning I lay my requests
before you and wait in expectation.

Psalm 27:14   Wait for the Lord; be strong and take
heart and wait for the Lord.

Psalm 37:4   Delight yourself in the Lord and he will
give you the desires of your heart.

Psalm 121:3   He will not let your foot slip—he who
watches over you will not slumber;
indeed, he who watches over Israel
will neither slumber nor sleep.

Jeremiah 31:3   The Lord appeared to us in the past, saying: "I have loved you with an ever-lasting love; I have drawn you with loving-kindness."

Romans 8:38–39   For I am convinced that neither death nor life, neither angels nor demons, neither the present nor the future, nor any powers, neither height nor depth, nor anything else in all creation, will be able to separate us from the love of God that is in Christ Jesus our Lord.

YOU FEEL AFRAID

Psalm 27:1   The Lord is my light and my salvation—whom shall I fear? The Lord is the stronghold of my life—of whom shall I be afraid?

Psalm 91:9–12   If you make the Most High your dwelling—even the Lord, who is my refuge—then no harm will befall you, no disaster will come near your tent. For he will command his angels concerning you to guard you in all your ways; they will lift you up in their hands, so that you will not strike your foot against a stone.

Psalm 91:14–15   "Because he loves me," says the Lord,
"I will rescue him; I will protect him,
for he acknowledges my name. He will
call upon me, and I will answer him; I
will be with him in trouble, I will
deliver him and honor him."

Psalm 118:6–7   The Lord is with me; I will not be
afraid. What can man do to me? The
Lord is with me; he is my helper. I will
look in triumph on my enemies.

Isaiah 41:10   So do not fear, for I am with you; do not
be dismayed, for I am your God. I will
strengthen you and help you; I will
uphold you with my righteous right
hand.

Nahum 1:7   The Lord is good, a refuge in times of
trouble. He cares for those who trust
in him.

John 14:27   Peace I leave with you; my peace I
give you. I do not give to you as the
world gives. Do not let your hearts be
troubled and do not be afraid.

*Philippians
4:12–13*   I know what it is to be in need, and I
know what it is to have plenty. I have

learned the secret of being content in any and every situation, whether well fed or hungry, whether living in plenty or in want. I can do everything through him who gives me strength.

Hebrews 13:6   So we say with confidence, "The Lord is my helper; I will not be afraid. What can man do to me?"

YOU FEEL TEMPTED

Psalm 119:11   I have hidden your word in my heart that I might not sin against you.

Proverbs 28:20   A faithful man will be richly blessed, but one eager to get rich will not go unpunished.

John 14:15   If you love me, you will obey what I command.

Acts 24:16   So I strive always to keep my conscience clear before God and man.

Romans 12:1–2   Therefore, I urge you, brothers, in view of God's mercy, to offer your bodies as living sacrifices, holy and pleasing to God—this is your spiritual act of worship. Do not conform any longer to the pattern of this world, but be transformed by the renewing of your mind. Then you will be able to test and approve what God's will is—his good, pleasing and perfect will.

1 Corinthians 6:19–20

Do you not know that your body is a temple of the Holy Spirit, who is in you, whom you have received from God? You are not your own; you were bought at a price. Therefore honor God with your body.

1 Corinthians 10:13

No temptation has seized you except what is common to man. And God is faithful; he will not let you be tempted beyond what you can bear. But when you are tempted, he will also provide a way out so that you can stand up under it.

Ephesians 5:8

For you were once darkness, but now you are light in the Lord. Live as children of light.

James 1:12

Blessed is the man who perseveres under trial, because when he has stood the test, he will receive the crown of life that God has promised to those who love him.

1 John 4:4	You, dear children, are from God and have overcome them (the spirits of the world), because the one who is in you is greater than the one who is in the world.

YOU FEEL ANXIOUS

Matthew 6:19–21	Do not store up for yourselves treasures on earth, where moth and rust destroy, and where thieves break in and steal. But store up for yourselves treasures in heaven, where moth and rust do not destroy, and where thieves do not break in and steal. For where your treasure is, there your heart will be also.
Luke 12:11–12	When you are brought before synagogues, rulers, and authorities, do not worry about how you will defend yourselves or what you will say, for the Holy Spirit will teach you at that time what you should say.
Luke 12:25–26	Who of you by worrying can add a single hour to his life? Since you cannot

do this very little thing, why do you worry about the rest?

Philippians 4:6–7 Do not be anxious about anything, but in everything, by prayer and petition, with thanksgiving, present your requests to God. And the peace of God, which transcends all understanding, will guard your hearts and your minds in Christ Jesus.

1 Peter 5:7 Cast all your anxiety on him because he cares for you.

YOU ARE GRIEVING

Jeremiah 10:19b Yet I said to myself, "This is my sickness, and I must endure it."

Matthew 5:4 Blessed are those who mourn, for they will be comforted.

Romans 8:26–28 In the same way, the Spirit helps us in our weakness. We do not know what we ought to pray for, but the Spirit himself intercedes for us with groans that words cannot express and he who searches our hearts knows the mind of the Spirit, because the Spirit intercedes for the saints in accordance with God's will. And we know that in all things God works for the good of those who love him, who have been called according to his purpose.

2 Corinthians 1:3–4

Praise be to the God and Father of our Lord Jesus Christ, the Father of compassion and the God of all comfort, who comforts us in all our troubles, so that we can comfort those in any trouble with the comfort we ourselves have received from God.

1 Thessalonians 4:13–14

Brothers, we do not want you to be ignorant about those who fall asleep, or to grieve like the rest of men, who have no hope. We believe that Jesus died and rose again and so we believe that God will bring with Jesus those who have fallen asleep in him.

John 11:35

Jesus wept.

YOU FEEL DISCOURAGED

Psalm 23:1

The Lord is my shepherd, I shall not be in want.

Psalm 42:5, 11   Why are you downcast, O my soul? Why so disturbed within me? Put your hope in God, for I will yet praise him, my Savior and my God.

Psalm 55:17–18   Evening, morning and noon I cry out in distress, and he hears my voice. He ransoms me unharmed from the battle waged against me, even though many oppose me.

Philippians 4:8   Finally, brothers, whatever is true, whatever is noble, whatever is right, whatever is pure, whatever is lovely, whatever is admirable—if anything is excellent or praiseworthy—think about such things.

Matthew 5:11–12   Blessed are you when people insult you, persecute you and falsely say all kinds of evil against you because of me. Rejoice and be glad, because great is your reward in heaven, for in the same way they persecuted the prophets who were before you.

John 10:10   The thief comes only to steal and kill and destroy; I have come that they may have life, and have it to the full.

Hebrews 6:10

God is not unjust; he will not forget your work and the love you have shown him as you have helped his people and continue to help them.

YOU NEED TO MAKE A DECISION

Hosea 6:3

Let us acknowledge the Lord; let us press on to acknowledge him. As surely as the sun rises, he will appear; he will come to us like the winter rains, like the spring rains that water the earth.

1 Corinthians 9:24–25

Do you not know that in a race all the runners run, but only one gets the prize? Run in such a way as to get the prize. Everyone who competes in the games goes into strict training. They do it to get a crown that will not last; but we do it to get a crown that will last forever.

Philippians 3:13b–14

But one thing I do: Forgetting what is behind and straining toward what is ahead, I press on toward the goal to win the prize for which God has called me heavenward in Christ Jesus.

James 1:5–6

If any of you lacks wisdom, he should ask God, who gives generously to all without finding fault, and it will be given to him. But when he asks, he must believe and not doubt, because he who doubts is like a wave of the sea, blown and tossed by the wind.

YOU ARE IN PAIN

Psalm 6:2

Be merciful to me, Lord, for I am faint; O Lord, heal me, for my bones are in agony.

Psalm 42:11

Why are you downcast, O my soul? Why so disturbed within me? Put your hope in God, for I will yet praise him, my Savior and my God.

Matthew 26:39

Going a little farther, he fell with his face to the ground and prayed, "My Father, if it is possible, may this cup be taken from me. Yet not as I will, but as you will."

Mark 9:23–24

"'If you can'?" said Jesus. "Everything is possible for him who believes." Immediately the boy's father exclaimed, "I do believe; help me overcome my unbelief!"

2 Corinthians 12:9 But he said to me, "My grace is sufficient for you, for my power is made
perfect in weakness."

James 5:13 Is anyone of you in trouble? He should
pray. Is anyone happy? Let him sing
songs of praise.

YOU WONDER HOW TO RESPOND TO THE NEEDY

*Leviticus
25:35–37* If one of your countrymen becomes
poor and is unable to support himself
among you, help him as you would an
alien or temporary resident, so he can
continue to live among you. Do not
take interest of any kind from him, but
fear your God, so that your country-
man may continue to live among you.
You must not lend him money at interest or sell him food at a profit.

*Deuteronomy
15:11* There will always be poor people in the
land. Therefore I command you to be
openhanded toward your brothers and
toward the poor and needy in your land.

*Deuteronomy
24:14–15* Do not take advantage of a hired man
who is poor and needy, whether he is a
brother Israelite or an alien living in

one of your towns. Pay him his wages each day before sunset, because he is poor and is counting on it.

———

Proverbs 3:27 Do not withhold good from those who deserve it, when it is in your power to act.

———

Proverbs 14:31 He who oppresses the poor shows contempt for their Maker, But whoever is kind to the needy honors God.

———

Proverbs 17:5 He who mocks the poor shows contempt for their Maker; Whoever gloats over disaster will not go unpunished.

———

Proverbs 19:17 He who is kind to the poor lends to the Lord, and he will reward him for what he has done.

90 Days to Wisdom and Praise

The spiritual discipline of reading the Bible is critical in the life of the believer since it is our personal connection to God's Word. The more often we connect, the more often we will experience the power of God's Word in our lives.

The Bible is a collection of sixty-six books—a library—and contains a singular story. I want to encourage you to methodically read through the library to capture the complete story of the Book of God. Probably only a small portion of people actually succeed in reading through the whole Bible in a year. So what I am suggesting is a more manageable project. Why not devote a three-month period to read the highlights of the Bible so you get the big picture?

I've outlined God's book in the following Bible reading plan to show the main borders that hold the puzzle together:

- Creation, Beginnings
- The Fall, Human Separation from God, Evil Reigns
- Rebellion
- Redemption
- Restoration
- Discipleship, Service
- The Second Coming, Eternity

I have tried to include in each section a variety of Scripture passages—Old Testament and New Testament as well as the poetry of Proverbs and the Psalms.

The goal of this reading is for you to understand the message of the Bible and know what God is personally saying to you. As you read, place yourself in the text just as if you were there. In that scenario, you might ask the following questions of your experience:

- Where did I come from? (or How did I get into this story?)
- Why am I here? (or What is God's purpose for me in this story?) and, finally,
- Where am I going? (or What decisions do I need to make and where will those decisions take me?)

Select a translation of the Bible that is accurate and readable. For many years I have bought a new Bible to read through at the beginning of the year. I write the starting date on the front fly page, then when I have finished reading through, it is a milestone to write the completion date on the back fly page! (Hey, what can I say? I am goal driven.) Schedule a time on a daily basis for your Bible reading, just as you schedule meal times and appointments. Find an accountability partner, a friend who will have the boldness and your permission to simply ask from time to time "Did you read the Bible today?" Your response can be either "Yes" or "Not yet!" You may even want to find a group of people with whom you can meet to discuss the Bible passages you are reading together. Perhaps if you are part of a small group in your church you can suggest that the group undertake this 90-day reading plan together and make it part of your discussions. Such discussions may help you build into your daily reading a deeper level of comprehension.

Pray, seeking the Holy Spirit's intervention into your time alone with God and his Word. Remember, the goal is not the number of pages, chapters, or books you read. If the Holy Spirit says, "Stop and ponder, meditate on this passage," stop and do that. Let the Word of God speak directly to you.

So let's begin with the book of Genesis, which is probably the one book of the Bible with which we are most familiar. Many of us start out on January 1 of each year by opening our Bible to Genesis 1:1, though most of us don't make it to the fifteenth of the month! As you begin now to read the account of creation and the many stories of beginnings, consider the fact that the book of Genesis is a summary account of the entire Bible. You will read about relationships, the one and only true God, and even the definition of faith (Genesis 15:6). If you get hung up on the list of names, ask yourself where your name might appear in that genealogy if it were to continue into this generation. (Wouldn't it be cool to have your name in the Bible?) As you begin, some of the passages are a bit long, but you have read the stories before, so it shouldn't be too tough. Hang in there.

THE CREATION, BEGINNINGS

Day 1   *Genesis 1–2*   Date: _____

Day 2   *Psalm 33*   Date: _____

Day 3   *Psalm 145*   Date: _____

Day 4	*Genesis 5–9*	Date: _____
Day 5	*Genesis 10–15*	Date: _____
Day 6	*Genesis 16–19*	Date: _____
Day 7	*Genesis 20–25*	Date: _____
Day 8	*Genesis 26–36*	Date: _____
Day 9	*Genesis 37–41*	Date: _____
Day 10	*Genesis 42–45,* *Psalms 89–90*	Date: _____
Day 11	*Genesis 46–50,* *Psalm 119:1–16*	Date: _____

Congratulations. You have made it through creation and the beginning of time. As you now continue on your journey through the story of God in the Bible, you will read about the first sin, about human separation from God because of that sin and how sin continued—and continues—to reign. The daily passages are a bit shorter in this section. That will allow you time to pray more! Pray that Satan will be bound, and you will not be separated from God.

THE FALL, HUMAN SEPARATION FROM GOD, EVIL REIGNS

Day 12   *Genesis 3*   Date: _____

Day 13   *Genesis 4*   Date: _____

Day 14   *Genesis 6*   Date: _____

Day 15   *Job 31*   Date: _____

Day 16   *Hosea 4*   Date: _____

Day 17   *Isaiah 65: 1–16*   Date: _____

Day 18   *Psalm 14*   Date: _____

Day 19   *Psalm 51*   Date: _____

Day 20   *Psalm 58*   Date: _____

Day 21   *Matthew 12–13*   Date: _____

Day 22   *Romans 1:18–3:20*   Date: _____

Day 23   *Jude*   Date: _____

Day 24   Psalm 94   Date: _____

Day 25   Isaiah 1   Date: _____

By now, you have been reading the Bible on a daily basis for nearly a month. Congratulations. For most people it takes only four more days for daily Bible reading discipline to become a life-long habit. But be warned, sin reigns and the rebellion of Satan is ready to attack and disrupt your spiritual growth and discipline. Allow the following passages about the rebellion of human beings toward God to strengthen you and give you the fortitude to defeat Satan. Oh, and have you checked in with your accountability partner? If yes, great. If not, give an update today.

REBELLION

Day 26   Exodus 4:1–5:4   Date: _____

Day 27   Exodus 8–9   Date: _____

Day 28   Exodus 10–11   Date: _____

Day 29   Psalm 10   Date: _____

Day 30   Proverbs 20   Date: _____

Day 31   *Proverbs 21*   Date: _____

Day 32   *Numbers 14*   Date: _____

Day 33   *Deuteronomy 13*   Date: _____

Day 34   *Jonah 1–4*   Date: _____

Day 35   *Jeremiah 5*   Date: _____

Day 36   *Ezekiel 18*   Date: _____

Day 37   *Hosea 10*   Date: _____

Day 38   *Micah 2*   Date: _____

Day 39   *1 Timothy 1*   Date: _____

Wow, the rebellion of man is bad stuff! Now the story of God begins to get really good. There is hope for each one of us. People in our culture and time have connected with God's Word and been redeemed. You have read twenty-one stories of such incidents. Now you can go to the source of the redemption story that is found throughout the Bible. Don't forget to ask yourself where you are in the following passages of Scripture.

REDEMPTION

Day 40   Exodus 12   Date: _____

Day 41   Leviticus 16   Date: _____

Day 42   Ruth 1–4   Date: _____

Day 43   Hebrews 9–10   Date: _____

Day 44   Psalm 49   Date: _____

Day 45   Luke 1–2   Date: _____

Day 46   Romans 2–4   Date: _____

Day 47   Colossians 1–2   Date: _____

Day 48   Luke 13   Date: _____

Day 49   1 Peter 1–2   Date: _____

Day 50   Revelation 5   Date: _____

Day 51   John 3   Date: _____

Day 52   Isaiah 53   Date: _____

Day 53   Matthew 26–28   Date: _____

Day 54   Matthew 1   Date: _____

Day 55   Romans 11   Date: _____

The power of God's Word is evident in lives changed and restored to a loving and eternal relationship with God. As you read through these sections of the Bible, take time to praise God for the restoration he has brought in the lives of people in the Bible, in history, in our day, and in your life. In the following passages, you will read how people sought restoration with God.

RESTORATION

Day 56   Psalm 80   Date: _____

Day 57   Lamentations 5   Date: _____

Day 58   Psalm 23   Date: _____

Day 59   Acts 3   Date: _____

Day 60   2 Corinthians 13   Date: _____

Day 61   Revelation 21   Date: _____

Day 62   1 John 3   Date: _____

Day 63   Psalm 5   Date: _____

Day 64   Psalm 32   Date: _____

Day 65   Jeremiah 31   Date: _____

Day 66   John 9   Date: _____

Day 67   Psalm 51   Date: _____

As people through the ages have come to faith in Christ and a restored relationship to their heavenly Father, they have responded by building on their faith and by serving God. As you read the following passages of the Bible, reflect on your spiritual growth as God's Word has nourished you over the past two months. Consider how you are serving God through your family, work, and church. Do you need to make changes? Reflect on people of the Bible and how they made decisions to do what God wanted them to do. And ask yourself, Why am I here?

DISCIPLESHIP, SERVICE

Day 68   Numbers 5–6   Date: _____

Day 69   Joshua 24   Date: _____

Day 70   Deuteronomy 10–11 Date: _____

Day 71   1 Samuel 12   Date: _____

Day 72   Matthew 6   Date: _____

Day 73   Luke 9   Date: _____

Day 74   John 13   Date: _____

Day 75   Acts 2   Date: _____

Day 76   Acts 8   Date: _____

Day 77   Romans 14–15   Date: _____

Day 78   1 Corinthians 12–13 Date: _____

Day 79   Philippians 1–2   Date: _____

Day 80   Revelation 2–3   Date: _____

The story of Creation is filled with wonder and awe. The stuff in between can be exciting but a bit depressing! The Bible tells us we will live forever. It gives us some detail about where that will be and what it will be like. It even helps us understand we have a choice of where! (Make sure you have made the right decision on this one.) As God's people, we can be assured we are heaven bound. As you finish this 90 days of reading your Bible, take time to thank God for the wisdom he has given you to make the right choice and praise him for your salvation. That is the most powerful connection we can make. Indeed, we are heaven bound.

THE SECOND COMING, ETERNITY

Day 81   Revelation 19–20, 22   Date: _____

Day 82   Romans 8   Date: _____

Day 83   Matthew 24–25   Date: _____

Day 84   Daniel 7–12   Date: _____

Day 85   Isaiah 63–66   Date: _____

Day 86   2 Thessalonians 2   Date: _____

Day 87   Romans 5–6   Date: _____

Day 88   John 5–6   Date: _____

Day 89   1 John 5   Date: _____

Day 90   Ecclesiastes 12   Date: _____

Congratulations. You have finished reading the overview of the story of God. Now, go back and fill in the parts of the Bible you skipped in the last 90 days. Keep up the good work of connecting with God's Word. May this be the beginning of your life-long discipline of reading the Bible every day until Jesus comes! And, don't forget to give Scripture sensitively and appropriately to others who are seeking spiritually.

Acknowledgments

Both of us are blessed by supportive family and friends who were our cheerleaders during the planning and writing of this book, especially Erin Moraine and Bonnie McGowan, who assisted us with endless details. Special thanks to Greg Johnson of Alive Communications, Inc. for introducing us to the Zondervan publishing team. We're especially appreciative of Executive Editor Paul Engle's thoughtful guidance during the process and the tracking of details by Angela Scheff, Associate Editor.

About the Authors

Thomas L. Youngblood joined the International Bible Society (IBS) in 1986. He passionately believes in and promotes the life-changing power of the Scriptures. His current role oversees the outreach efforts of IBS in the United States.

Tom's extensive and enthusiastic promotion of the Scriptures has resulted in the development of strategic partnerships with various ministries. His focus centers on providing appropriate Scripture resources to four major groups: children, disaster/crisis victims, emerging young leaders, and prison ministries.

Tom particularly enjoys serving at his church, Woodmen Valley Chapel in Colorado Springs, by helping children memorize Scripture and preparing the area's finest coffee drinks at the church's espresso bar!

He has completed the residency requirement on a doctorate in adult education, an M.A. in Education from Wheaton College, and a B.S. from Philadelphia Biblical University.

Sandra P. Aldrich, president and CEO of Bold Words, Inc., in Colorado Springs, is a popular speaker, author or coauthor of sixteen books, and contributing author to an additional dozen. Two of her most recent books—*Heart-Prints* and *Will I Ever Be Whole Again?*—were awarded Silver Angels by the Excellence in Media group.

Her other books include: *101 Upward Glances* (Focus on the Family/Tyndale), *Bless Your Socks Off* (Focus on the Family/Tyndale), *Men Read Newspapers, Not Minds*

(Tyndale), and *From One Single Mother to Another* (Regal Books, eleventh printing 2001).

Sandra is a frequent speaker at women's and couple's retreats, military gatherings, college conferences, hospice seminars, single-parent events, business meetings, and educational workshops where she presents the serious issues of life with insight and humor.

Her five hundred-plus articles have appeared in *Focus on the Family* magazine, *Moody Magazine, Today's Christian Woman,* and *Discipleship Journal,* among others.

She holds an M.F.A. degree from Eastern Michigan University, but says it is her "Ph.D. in the School of Hard Knocks" that makes her a much-in-demand guest on numerous TV and radio programs, including several *Focus on the Family* broadcasts. She also is the former senior editor of *Focus on the Family* magazine.

Send us your Bible encounter story:
Bible Encounters
P.O. Box 62428
Colorado Springs, CO 80962
Or email us your story at BoldWords@aol.com

We want to hear from you. Please send your comments about this book to us in care of the address below. Thank you.

GRAND RAPIDS, MICHIGAN 49530 USA

WWW.ZONDERVAN.COM